Historic Tales
of
SYLVA AND
JACKSON COUNTY

Historic Tales

of

SYLVA AND
JACKSON COUNTY

Jim Buchanan

THE
History
PRESS

Published by The History Press
Charleston, SC
www.historypress.com

Copyright © 2020 by Jim Buchanan
All rights reserved

Front cover, bottom: *Sketch by Julie Buchanan.*

First published 2020

Manufactured in the United States

ISBN 9781467145756

Library of Congress Control Number: 2020930493

These stories are dedicated to Howard and Brittie Buchanan, Vivien, Howard Jr., Gary, Connie, Cathy and the characters and salt-of-the-earth folks of Jackson County.

Contents

Acknowledgements 11
Introduction 13

1. A-Hunting We Will Go
Catch-22: Leave the Truck or Stay 17
The Plott Thickens 19
Slackness Vs. Stubbornness: A Breakin' Avoided 21
Once, Bullets Weren't Things to Waste 23
The Tracking Gift Was Something to Behold 25
The Tale of the Interstate Sandwich 28

2. A Walk Among the Flora and Fauna—but Mostly Snakes
The Dirt on Modern Lawns 31
The Fiercest Beast in the Mountains 33
A Bovine with Death on His Mind 34
A Bit of Horse Sense on the Economy 37
Nothing Divine About This Vine 39
Fresh Fish, Straight from the Box 41
The Dark Saga of the Republican Beans 43
Turtles, and History, on the Move 44
This Particular Possum Wasn't Playing 46
The Fine Art of Mountain Angling 47
Snakes Don't Take Off for Labor Day 49
Close Encounters of the Furred Kind 51
More Snakes Come Out of the Woodwork 53

CONTENTS

3. MOUNTAIN CHARACTER, MOUNTAIN CHARACTERS
Technology Unwinds Some Old Traditions of Watch
    Pockets and Pocket Watches   57
Granny Was Up to Snuff When It Came to Bee Stings   58
Humor Gene Came from Some Special Ladies   60
Hillbilly Upbringing Has Its Pitfalls: An Inadvertent Lesson
    in Sensitivity Training   62
At One Logging Camp, a Near-Fatal Dose of Gravy   64
Explosive Tales and a One-of-a-Kind Hobby   68
Learning to Drive Involved Moments of Sheer Terror   70
Itching for a Visit from an Old Nemesis   71
A Time When Phones Were a Party   74
Patching Together a Look at Some Fashion No-Nos   75
When Disaster Strikes, Sometimes It's Best to Not
    Pick Up the Phone   77
Maybe It's Time to Bring Graft Back   78
Love of Sports Veered into Dangerous Territory   81
Signs of the (Forgotten) Times   83
A Cool Mountain Spot When the Heat Is On   85
Sharp Edges and Dull Minds   87
Maybe We Should Tackle Litter Differently: Sometimes
    the Better Angels of Our Nature Just Don't Show Up   89
A Winner in the "Sweep" Stakes   92

4. MOVING THROUGH THE YEAR
Rewards of Rail-Splitting Were Elusive   95
Going Batty Over a Burst of Wild Onions   97
Plowing Time: From Tractor to Tiller to Mule   99
The Little Egg That Could…Lead to a Car Crash   101
Ramping Up for Easter; Ham and a Mountain Necessity   102
Puttin' Up Time Comes Again to the Mountains   103
Some Fundamental Shifts in the Culture: Who Knew
    Lightnin' Bugs Would Become an Economic Driver?   106
There's Something in the Air, so Beware   107
I Couldn't Stand the Heat, so I Did in Fact Get
    Out of the Kitchen   109
The Garden Ends, Mayhem Begins   111
The Season of Omens and Portents   112

CONTENTS

It Slices, It Dices—No Wait, It Just Empties Your
    Bank Account   114
Yes, It's Cold, but It Still Beats the Heat   115
Tales of Turkey Terror   117
Coping (or Not) with the Snows of Old   119
Orange Memories with a Side of Rice   120
Cloak and Dagger Time Arrived with Christmas   122
The Powerful Pull of Mountain Home   124

About the Author   127

Acknowledgements

Grateful thanks go out to the good folks at the Sylva Herald for indulging me for so long, the great editing and proofing of the Herald gang, Jason Brady at Western Carolina University's Hunter Library and all those who have shared their stories and encouragement along the way.

Our family has deep roots in the Buchanan, Deitz and Cabe families of Jackson County, and large family gatherings always came with stories of the old folks and the old folkways. Along the way, the family created stories of its own, and the stories retold were tales that almost always had a humorous side. Frankly, the old stories are a lot more interesting than the tales a lot of us are crafting today, living in an age when we're tied down, Gulliver-like, to our devices.

The Appalachians are steeped in a wonderful tradition of oral history. The pitfall of oral histories, however, is that when people pass away, they often take their stories with them.

So, as time went by, I decided to write them down. I encourage others to do the same. I truly do believe everyone has a book in them.

I hope this book can be a spark for others to share their stories.

And, if nothing else, good for a few laughs.

Introduction

October was a big, big month in the Buchanan household on East Fork. For me, the turning of the calendar started the countdown toward Halloween—second only to Christmas as far as holidays went. For my father, Howard Tatham Buchanan—henceforth referred to as Daddy, the name he wanted his children to call him, a request I intend to honor—October was bigger than Christmas, Halloween, the Fourth of July and his own birthday combined.

October marked the start of bear season. And with bear hunts come stories.

Some years back, Daddy and Arthur Dillard were off on a hunt, where they parked deep in the woods of the Tellico area near the Tennessee–North Carolina line. In this particular story, Daddy and Arthur found a bear track and turned the dogs on it. I gathered that they walked a good way before they found the track and chased the pack pursuing the bear another considerable distance.

As was the most common outcome in those days, the chase didn't yield a kill. Thus they found themselves miles and miles from where they'd parked. They'd set up a rendezvous point with another hunter, where he would pick them up. But the timing for that meeting was around 3:00 p.m., and they only made it back to that spot as the sun was setting.

Mountain miles are hard to traverse, but there are times when there's no option but to do so, and this was one of those times. They started walking and walking and walking, with dogs on their leashes in tow.

Daddy peeking out from behind a bear hung for slaughter. While putting up a bird feeder is about all it takes to encounter a bear these days, forty years ago, it involved going deep into the wilds, and more often than not, the day might end without so much as a rumor of a bear. *Author's collection.*

They struck a dirt road, and around midnight they came upon a house with the porch light on. There Daddy saw an option that might end the forced march. He offered Arthur twenty dollars if he'd go up, knock on the door and see if they could get a ride. Now, twenty dollars was worth considerably more in those days than today, but I'm guessing that Daddy was thinking it was a good bargain.

This could save them hours of walking. And, in the event things went south, I suppose he'd rather see Arthur get shot than himself. I guess he'd get to keep the twenty dollars as a bonus.

To everyone's surprise, Arthur took the deal. He went to the porch and knocked. A housewife in a nightgown opened the door.

As Arthur put it, "Hell, I don't know what I was thinking. I just said the first thing that came to my mind: 'Ma'am, how'd you like to make twenty dollars?'"

They did not get a ride.

Apparently, the house shook from the force of the door being jacked in Arthur's face. Daddy, down in the road holding the dogs, was laughing his tail off.

They made it back to the truck and got out of that country around sunrise.

I heard this story while sitting with Daddy at the hospice center at the Charles George VA Medical Center in Asheville, about a month shy of his ninetieth birthday and three weeks before his passing. Arthur had been to the VA for a session and had swung by to see Daddy. The folks at the VA treated him exceptionally well, and he had a lot of visitors.

I'd always considered putting these stories down on paper, but I think it was this tale that sealed the deal. My oldest brother, Howard Buchanan Jr., delivered this one, along with a lot of other stories, during the eulogy at Daddy's funeral. It still ranks as the finest eulogy I've ever heard.

And so begins this collection of mountain stories.

They will represent a slice of time from a generation departed—bits and pieces of history from a Western North Carolina that has drastically changed over the years as the old mountain people died off and the hills began filling up with outsiders.

I do not consider the tales my own, but I'm the one telling them. I'm sure some of the details are probably off. Maybe others can share their own tales and fill in the blanks at a later date. At any rate, they are stories worth telling. So, here we go.

1

A-Hunting We Will Go

CATCH-22: LEAVE THE TRUCK OR STAY

Apocalypse Now has the famous line "never leave the boat." With me, it was "never leave the truck."

If you left the truck with Daddy on a bear hunt, there was literally no telling where you'd wind up. You might be miles deep in the woods with no rendezvous set up. You might be near exhaustion with many miles already under your belt when he finally turned on a bear, and there was no turning back once that started.

Staying in the truck meant you'd at least have a ride home. That option, though, also had its downsides.

Daddy was hard on trucks. More to the point, the country he took his trucks into was hard on trucks. A broken axle was pretty much his signature pitch. Most of the time, though, the trucks were running, albeit with the rearview mirrors broken off and an electrical short or two.

In more extreme versions, he'd turn a truck into a National Transportation Safety Board exhibit. One year, we almost lost my friend Geoff Cantrell when the passenger door popped open on Rufus Ray curve.

Quite often the dashboard lights would short out. We'd be weaving through the Nantahala Gorge in predawn darkness, and he'd pick up a flashlight to see how fast he was going. He wasn't checking to see if he was speeding. He knew good and well he was speeding. He was just mildly curious to see by how much.

"How much" makes an…exhilarating…difference in the Gorge.

Now, Daddy was a law-abiding man. But like most mountain people of his generation, he had little tolerance for rules that didn't make any sense. If the speed limit sign said twenty-five miles per hour but you could go forty-five, you went forty-five. There were places to go and bears to kill.

It wasn't his skirting the rules of the road that made him stand out, though, it was his contempt for the laws of physics.

In his later years, there were stories of hunters needing rides after long days in the woods who would hide in the bushes when they heard him coming. As he'd powerslide past their position, they'd reemerge more than happy to just keep walking.

He knew the size of a sapling that he could run over on an overgrown trail without stalling the truck. He'd take a truck around or over any obstacle between himself and a bear. Many times, he'd hit an old, long-abandoned logging road that had been washed out to the point that no one else would even consider giving it a try. From time to time, the truck would pretty much be vertical. I recall one time we'd gone so far to the right that he was driving from the passenger seat, which was disturbing because (a) I was still in it and

Most people would be hesitant to start up a road like this. Daddy would see it and calculate that it was pretty steep but had no major trees or gullies in the middle of it. He might make the decision to drop down into third gear but probably not. *Courtesy Dave Russell.*

(b) he was only able to reach the pedals with his left foot, which is not an ideal operating plan when driving a straight shift.

Still, he always pulled it off. He'd go up a skid trail, and he'd go up a spot where someone had considered a skid trail and decided it was too steep. Actually, saying he always pulled it off is a bit of a stretch.

When he didn't, well, at least he helped keep America's axle industry healthy.

THE PLOTT THICKENS

To many people in this area, the name Plott is immediately recognizable. For others, it might require a bit of ruminating.

"Plott. Plott. Now where have I heard that?"

Ah. The Plott hound, North Carolina's official state dog. Bob Plott is the namesake of the Plotts, whose name is forever linked to the renowned hunting dogs. He's a third great-grandson of Johannes George Plott, who brought the breed to the New World in the mid-eighteenth century and was a great-great-nephew of Henry Plott, who introduced the breed to the Smokies.

Bob Plott crafted an entertaining read with his book *Plott Hound Tales: Legendary People & Places behind the Breed*. In short, Plott relates the tremendous respect hunters have for Plott hounds, long famed for their tirelessness, fierceness in a bear or hog fight, intelligence and tracking ability. He weaves tales of legendary dogs, legendary hunters and legendary bears.

He takes a look at hunters such as Ed Watkins, "6 foot and 3 inches of muscle and brawn and 190 pounds of pure hate," and tells the tale of Honest John, a 700-pound bear that would eat only pork and would take only one kill at a time, usually a farmer's prized hog. He writes of Honest John's decades-long pursuer, Wilburn Parker, who speculated that Honest John was the lone survivor of a bear litter wiped out by a boar and thus set out on a life of revenge.

The Plott line is rooted in Haywood County and is beloved in Jackson—a fair trade, as a lot of hunters from Jackson County strayed into the country surrounding us for bear hunts, including my late father. Daddy could find his way in and out of places like the Nantahala Gorge and Hornbuckle blindfolded, which was handy, as he often found himself in pitch-black darkness after a hunt.

Daddy with one of his beloved Plott hounds, standing in front of a shed thrown up in one day to handle slaughtering a hog. It later became home to the flotsam and jetsam of a life hunting and working construction. *Author's collection.*

Daddy ran these mountains with Brysons and Crowes and Queens and many others, most of whom favored Plott hounds. He had some of the finest dogs around and would be offered considerable sums to part with one, but he wasn't much of a dog dealer. He was lucky in life and rich in friends, but his luck with dogs was a bit askew; invariably, after a rich offer, the dog in question would fall prey to a boar, a cliff or the grille of a leaf looker.

Still, he loved his dogs, and they loved him. When not hunting, they were remarkably gentle. Old Boney, as mean a fighter as there was, could be found sunning himself off the back porch after a hunt, with the housecat's litter snoozing on top of him.

Plott's book takes readers back to the day of hard times and hard people—a time when no self-respecting barn went unadorned with a bearskin or at least a couple of coonskins, fruit of the Plotts' labor.

The book, for whatever reason, makes me think of a different bestseller of late, J.D. Vance's *Hillbilly Elegy.* Vance's Appalachia, Kentucky and Ohio, is a truly awful place full of addiction and disappointment and short on opportunity and dreams. Vance escaped, joined the marines and got an Ivy League degree. Good for him.

I wonder what made these two versions of Appalachia so different. Growing up here, sure, there were kids who wanted to get out and see the world or go off and make the big bucks, but most wanted to stay, and most did. And quite a few who went off to earn fame and fortune came back.

At times I wonder if we were the beneficiary of a geological jackpot of sorts. Vance was in coal country. The coal industry has been romanticized quite a bit of late as some kind of economic cure-all. Tennessee Ernie Ford sang of quite a different version—one that I suspect rings a bit more historically true.

The fact is, after watching West Virginia let many of its mountains get flat-top haircuts to get to the coal, with the refuse being dumped in adjoining streams, I'm quite happy there isn't coal under the Balsams, where the Plott hounds ran and still run today.

SLACKNESS VS. STUBBORNNESS: A BREAKIN' AVOIDED

Daddy abandoned me as a child.

I mean, repeatedly, about every ten days or so. It was a side effect of two things: his stubbornness and my slackness. Over the years, I've come to the conclusion that when those two attitudes clash, and slackness is going to win nine times out of ten.

Daddy was a big bear hunter. Aside from some religious mystics, I've never seen anyone as dedicated to something as he was to chasing bear.

Understand, these days were different. You had to go deep, deep into the woods to get on a bear track. Bears were few and were very wary of humans. You had to drive for miles and then walk for miles and know a lot of woodcraft just to put yourself in the same zip code as a bear. In other words, you had to take a great many steps that can now be replicated by the simple act of putting up a bird feeder.

Ta-da! Instant bear.

Anyway, Daddy could flow through the woods like water up until he was in his seventies. Somewhere along the line, he picked up the habit of "breaking" young hunters—running them until they were mentally, physically and spiritually exhausted. He did it to my two older brothers, at least one brother-in-law and countless other unsuspecting, young, wannabe sportsmen.

The ideal place to go limp is one where you're not liable to roll off a cliff if you fall asleep. This spot would do nicely. *Hunter Library, Western Carolina University.*

Bear season ran a limited time, but that didn't keep him out of the woods. No, there were dogs to be trained, and possums and coons to be pursued.

There were also hunters to be broken.

That's when my turn came around. But I had an ace up my sleeve: the art of giving up. I'm pretty sure I developed it due to my exposure to higher math. When Savannah, Sylva and Webster schools merged into Fairview, I was tossed into computer class. I didn't get it—didn't come close. In high school, algebra was even worse. In college, well, I'd still be in college trying to pass Algebra I if they hadn't stuck me in a remedial math summer class in order to be rid of me. I realized that when it came to math, I'd never get it, so my time was better spent giving up and doing something else.

Using this same line of reasoning, after Daddy would run me up and down and around the mountains working up to a good breakin', I'd just give up, sit down and go limp—full Gandhi. I think it drove him slightly insane because that was not the point. At all.

But after a few rounds of this, because there were still coons to be trailed and dogs to be trained and caught, he'd just leave me there. I'd curl up in my coat—generally two sizes too big, either because it was a hand-me-down or purchased that way, so I'd grow into it—and listen to the sounds of the forest at night. Those were wonderfully contemplative moments, catching a glimpse of a shooting star or pondering the sound of a motor far off in the distance and wondering who would be out at such an hour.

These incidents generally occurred when it was too cold for snakes to be out, and I was never afraid of anything else in the woods, so I developed a peace at being alone on some hillside, which bordered on unhealthy, I guess.

I knew Daddy would always come back. And he always did.

Besides, this was before bears were comfortable around humans. Plus, I figured if a bear was around, too bad for the bear. They were on dangerous turf. Daddy was out there somewhere in the dark.

Once, Bullets Weren't Things to Waste

Aside from the obviously appalling aspects of the drumbeat of mass shootings, one thing about those affairs stands out to me: volume.

There's a difference—a big difference—between hunting culture, which has long thrived in Western North Carolina, and the gun culture, which has sprung up across the United States in the last three decades or so. A traditional hunter in these mountains didn't fill the air with lead, as he would be quite frugal when it came to expending ammunition. That frugality is reflected in a number of stories, some that I witnessed firsthand, some that I heard about from reliable sources and one in particular that I wonder about.

I don't recall Daddy ever doing much more than one or two rounds as far as target practice. Actually, he wasn't practicing, he was just sighting in his rifle. He killed his first six bears with six bullets—six head shots.

Once we were riding up a logging road searching for dogs lost from a chase when he spotted a grouse perched in a tree about fifty yards up the mountain. He reached behind the truck seat, pulled out his .303 and dropped it. If he'd hit the bird in the body with a big game shell, he would've basically vaporized it. In an awkward seated position pointing uphill, still behind the wheel, he shot the grouse through the neck and took home supper.

No wasted bullet, no wasted bird. I don't recall seeing a shot like that before or since.

One of the tales that really made the rounds about Daddy was when he killed a wild boar with no bullet at all. A pack of dogs had jumped the razorback, and after a fight where it had cut up a number of the dogs pretty badly, the boar was down and nearly expired when Daddy arrived on the scene. He dispatched it with his pocketknife. This created a great deal of

Looking down into the Oconaluftee Valley. Bear hunting in this region was a way of life. Not wasting ammunition was another. *Hunter Library, Western Carolina University.*

amusement among other hunters, who were offering comparisons to a Davy Crockett-esque feat, but Daddy said he simply didn't want to waste a bullet. And I believed him.

Now to the story I wonder about—a tale of frugality taken to extreme levels.

While camping in the Smokies with family a few years back, a gentleman from Alabama set up in a nearby campsite and, smelling the chili I was cooking, drifted over and struck up a conversation. We gave him some chili, which he appreciated, and he said I was a handy man to have in camp, which I appreciated.

He'd been solo camping around the area, which is not a bad way to spend time. We got to talking about spots he'd been to and how long he'd been doing this. He'd been doing it for a long time and told a tale he'd heard years ago from an old-timer in the Hazel Creek area who'd informally guided him to some good fishing spots.

The gentleman—very advanced in age—said he'd been born and raised in the area. He said when he was young, seven or so, his father would send him and his nine-year-old brother out into the woods with two "punkinballs"—large, solid lead shotgun loads. The instructions for the boys were simple: come back with a bear or don't come back at all.

As the story went, the boys devised a method where they'd tree a bear, and one would shoot up at it while the other watched from a way off to see if the shot fulfilled its intent. If it didn't, they had another punkinball, and at least the bear would have to puzzle a bit before picking which of the two targets to maul. Their method worked well and paid off handsomely. With the bear down, they'd go get their father, who would skin it and take the pelt to town. For each pelt, he got four punkinballs.

Surely that can't be true. Can it?

The Tracking Gift Was Something to Behold

As Thanksgiving rolls around, my thoughts turn to snow.

I wonder if I need to pause here and explain what that is.

Nah. Snow is something we once experienced in considerable amounts in these mountains, usually starting with the first good jolt of hog-killin' cold in November. Most years, I'd head out and comb through the nearby hills for the family Christmas tree, which I'd drag home through a few inches of freshly fallen snow. I do remember one year when it didn't snow, and I dragged the tree up East Fork Road. By the time I got home, I had a lovely trail of needles but not a whole lot of tree.

At any rate, snow wasn't much of a novelty a few decades ago, so you learned how to live with it and enjoy its upsides: days off from school, hiding the leaves you hadn't raked, among others. For me it had one big downside: It ruined my possible career as a tracker.

Sadly, when I was a wee lad, we had plenty of snow, and that's where I learned my tracking. As it turns out, any fool can follow a track in snow, and I got accustomed to doing so to the point that when there wasn't snow, I was essentially useless.

I'd be in the truck with Daddy trolling up an old logging road; he'd have a hand on the wheel and his head halfway out the window, staring intently at the cut bank looking for a sign of a bear crossing. He'd see some disturbed dirt, get out and start digging a narrative out of a track—species, direction, size, age of track and stuff like that.

All I ever saw was disturbed dirt. I could not tell what had disturbed the dirt. Perhaps a rock had dislodged and rolled down the slope. Perhaps a limb had fallen. Perhaps it had received news of a sick relative. I just could not tell what had disturbed that dirt so.

Daddy would point. I would stare. I'd stare hard enough to see individual dirt molecules, hard enough to see all the way to China, but I'd never see a track—just that upset dirt. Daddy tried his best, but that particular gift skipped a generation.

The thing is, when another experienced tracker was around, things would start getting out of hand almost immediately. Tracking is a skill. One-upmanship is also a skill. The ensuing back-and-forth of two trackers on a sign was something to behold.

"I'd say it crossed last night."

"Yep. About 250-pounder."

"Female."

"Blood type O negative."

"Headed west, probably toward Burningtown Gap."

"Slight limp."

"Registered Republican."

"Hasn't voted since '74, though."

Looking back over the years, I am beginning to suspect there was some slight embellishment lent to the depth of tracking skills among my hunting comrades. There was a keen competition, it would seem, when it came to tracking.

An example of a track I could spot. Mountain bear hunters were much more skilled and were able to spot a light disturbance in the soil and divine a great many things, such as the sex, weight and voter registration of a bear. I sometimes wonder if these claims were embellished. *Hunter Library, Western Carolina University.*

One incident I vividly recall was a time Daddy had packed me off with another hunter, although the details of what I was seeing didn't dawn on me until years later.

Miles deep in the woods, we crossed one of the countless little branches that network these mountains and came across a track that was so obvious even I could tell it was a bear. I was treated to the usual details—three-hundred-pounder, three hours old, second-degree Mason, that sort of stuff.

Then, as my fellow hunter was squatting by the track rattling off statistics, he began dreamily mashing his fingers into the mud this way then that way, keenly intent on something. At the time, I figured he was testing the soil for whatever extra clues it might yield, but as the years went by, it dawned on me that he wasn't doing that at all.

He was clearly mimicking the track. It makes me wonder how many times over the years he had sent a pack of hunters off on a decoy after he'd kept a real track to himself. I must admit, it was pretty clever.

Bet I could do that if there was snow on the ground.

THE TALE OF THE INTERSTATE SANDWICH

Lloyd Cowan passed away recently. He was one of the last scions of East Fork—people who knew the community in and out, the rocks that stood against the river of changing times and passed down knowledge of the people and culture of a mountain settlement.

Services for Lloyd were held January 23, 2018, on what would have been his ninety-sixth birthday. He put in a lot of years, generally had an enjoyable time and left the community a better place. It's a legacy any of us would be happy with.

Lloyd did a great deal of historical and genealogical research in his day, and that work was often overlooked. However, it will stand the test of time.

What Lloyd was much better known for was being a direct fellow. It wasn't exactly the equivalent of a fan dance when it came to making his views known, both in his comments and in the voluminous letters he'd write and distribute to various people and entities in the area. He sent me a few of those and dropped off a great many at Mother and Daddy's that I'd read later on.

Lloyd enjoyed coming to the house for a meal, which is no great surprise, given Mother's legendary cooking. But this story isn't about that. It's about

Left to right, standing: Beecher Dalton, John B. Ensley, Mr. Ward, Fred Buchanan, Lloyd Kennedy, Tolvin Ward, Lloyd Cowan. *Left to right, kneeling*: Howard Buchanan, Medford Deitz, little Howard Allman and Jimmy Allman. Cowan produced a bear sandwich that was probably the most well-traveled such item in history. Allman was involved in a tale of local politics and international intrigue involving bush beans. *Author's Collection.*

Lloyd providing food himself. Lloyd was a familiar sight on the old logging roads when I'd go bear hunting with Daddy. On one occasion, I'd been packed off into the woods by Daddy to try to cut a bruin off at the pass. This I did not do, and after wandering through the shrub for a time, I popped out onto a road. By and by, I came across Lloyd and his truck.

Lloyd was a great fan of bear meat and was eager to give the uninitiated a taste. On this day, he had some sandwiches he offered to me. I'd had bear before and had rarely enjoyed it. In my view, the whole thing about bear came down to the grease; if that wasn't treated to tamp down the wild taste, either through a marinade or cooking technique, you'd have a meal that was gamy to the point that you'd think it might fight its way out of your mouth and escape back to the woods.

I've held to that stance on grease to this day. At a fine restaurant one time, the waiter presented a steak and oohed and ahhed about how juicy it was. I opined that juice came from oranges, and that was, in fact, a pool of grease on the plate. Kinda went downhill from there.

Back to Lloyd. As fate would have it, my meal for the day was in the truck, and Daddy was in the truck, and the truck was undoubtedly in motion, so I had no idea if my lunch or my father were still in the same zip code, let alone hemisphere.

So, when Lloyd offered some bear sandwiches, I said, "Sure." ("Spare bear" is something of an alien concept these days. Times were very different then.)

The grub was delicious. I don't know if Lloyd did the cooking for this batch of bear or if it was someone else, but there wasn't a hint of greasy gaminess. It had a fine roast taste. Lloyd was tickled and sent me on my way with another sandwich.

The *Guinness World Records* doesn't have an entry for most well-traveled bear sandwich, but I'm sure that one was it. I probably bushwhacked another ten to fifteen miles with the wax paper–wrapped bear in my pocket before Daddy tracked me down and extricated me from the woods. It went another forty to fifty miles back to the house in Sylva and then on to my house in Clyde and my former job in Asheville.

From there, a food writer had a bite, and a couple of nibbles were sent off to that writer's colleagues in Raleigh and Greenville, South Carolina. Then Dave Russell, my current confederate in Sylva and former coconspirator in Asheville, got ahold of the sandwich. From there, it went to Atlanta to Russell's family, where he—and I'm quoting here—said, "I'm not sure how many people had a taste. But it was a bunch."

It was Lloyd's own version of the loaves and fishes. I never had a chance to tell him that story. But I imagine he's smiling about it today.

2

A Walk Among the Flora and Fauna— but Mostly Snakes

THE DIRT ON MODERN LAWNS

I didn't just rise to the bait. I breached like a whale. The year would have been 1967. The time would've been spring. It was time to mow.

"You," a sibling said, "are too little to mow."

"Am not."

"Are too," another sibling chimed in.

"Am not!"

"Are too. Leave this to the grownups."

"Nuh-uh, I'll show you!"

And I did. Wrestled that lawnmower all up and down the family yard, which, as we were in the mountains, was sort of like mowing the Matterhorn.

I showed them. I showed them for about twenty years, as it turned out. Once size and IQ requirements for mowing were set, they were set in stone at la casa Buchanan.

Lawns are one reason I'm not a big fan of spring and summer. Between the mowing and weed whacking and other various chores, we essentially lose a day a week until the leaves fall. I'm no gardener, but I don't begrudge gardeners. At least they get something to eat out of the experience. Lawns, I don't know. Maybe it's my childhood trauma, but when it comes to lawns, there has always lurked in the back of my mind this sneaking suspicion that we've been had.

In the course of human events, lawns are a relatively new development. Back in the castle era, trees were cut down and lawns were cropped close to keep intruders/barbarians/timeshare salesmen from sneaking up on you. A bit later on, lawns were a status symbol of the wealthy, as the time and labor required to get a lush, green, evenly trimmed lawn was hideously expensive. Later on, after the invention of the lawnmower, lawns began to spread across the United States, and they went into warp drive with the advent of the cookie-cutter housing developments that began springing up after World War II.

If you're old enough, you probably recall a radically different type of yard here in the mountains: dirt. You probably recall an aunt or grandma sweeping such a yard. You probably remember thinking to yourself, "Why sweep dirt?"

In the case of one beloved aunt, the explanation seemed pretty simple: It removed the, er, evidence of chickens in the yard. Families were big, and there were always kids crawling around, so it was a simple matter of hygiene.

Another reason I've heard put forth is that the dirt yard was a tradition brought to these shores from Africa. There, sweeping the yard would smooth the sand; smooth, swept sand is what you want if you're looking for a snake track. The yard would provide evidence that a creepy crawly had entered the old homestead.

While mountain people were practical and unafraid of borrowing anything that worked from any culture, I'm sticking with the chicken theory for the most part. Sure, there were plenty of snakes around the coves and hollows—and plenty of gaps and openings for them to get inside houses—but sweeping the yard wouldn't have helped track a snake. Mountain clay gets hard to the point that it could repel antiaircraft fire. You couldn't track an elephant on that stuff.

In the end, as with so many other things, you wonder if the old-timers weren't onto something. The dirt yard is as dead as the dodo, and we're all dealing with mower blades, trimmer string, fertilizer and the hundred or so other things that have taken the place of a simple straw broom.

'Tis the lot of our age. Gotta keep that yard neat and trimmed. To do otherwise would be to attract snakes—or timeshare salesmen.

The Fiercest Beast in the Mountains

I found myself lying in a laurel thicket wearing a three-piece suit. I'd come home from some fancy function or other at Western Carolina University to be immediately informed that our steer, Jake, had pulled another jailbreak from the pasture and was laying waste to a good chunk of East Fork.

I briefly considering changing before going out after him, but nah. I had corralled Jake quickly and repeatedly during his increasingly frequent crime sprees. I had this. Piece of cake.

Badly winded and a bit dizzy from the midsummer heat, I could hear Jake thrashing around in the thicket above me. I assessed the situation, wondering if I should start chasing him again and risk heatstroke. I was troubled by the idea crawling around in the back of my head that he was just wearing me down before moving in for the kill. Either way, I figured I was ahead of the game, as I was already dressed for the funeral.

In the end, I heard Jake move off through the brush until he was out of hearing range. I brushed myself off and wandered back toward the house, where I found Jake wolfing down a row of corn.

Of all the animals from my younger years, Jake was the best escape artist. OK, "artist" probably isn't the best term, as his tactics involved (a) going over a fence or (b) going through a fence. That bull preferred a direct approach.

Some animals do exhibit true escape talent. The current Buchanan household cat, Jupiter, is clearly trying to learn how to open the French door to the back porch. We have a stand near the door, and she'll get on it and jump onto the latch, attempting to work it back and forth. It's fun to watch, like seeing a politician trying to grasp the concept of truthfulness—a lot of sweat and not much in the way of results. We keep that door locked, just as a precaution.

I would point out that Jupiter is very energetic but not very smart. She has yet to figure out the actual cat door in the garage. If she develops opposable thumbs, maybe then I'll start worrying.

The animal that truly befuddled me with its abilities, and the one that gave me the worst mauling I've received from an animal in my life, well, it's embarrassing. Readers know what the stories are usually about: bears, bear dogs, wild boars, rattlesnakes. Real he-man outdoor life stuff.

Let me introduce you to Freckles, the toughest gerbil in, if not these fifty United States, at least the Lower Forty-Eight.

You have a kid; kids have pets. It's the natural order of things. I was not familiar with gerbils, and my first experience with them yielded three observations: They're cute, they eat a lot and they do a lot on the supply end of the food cycle after all that eating. Ignorance is bliss.

We had a nice sturdy cage for Freckles. We'd let Freckles out to play a lot, and Freckles didn't seem to mind the cage.

Back in those days, I did a lot of work on the computer late at night down in the basement near the room where Freckles's confinement was located. One night, I picked up something out of the corner of my eye—free-range Freckles.

I cornered Freckles, gave the cage a good looking over to make sure bars weren't bent and no opening had presented itself—I never did find one—and locked Freckles back up. A half hour later, I picked up something out the corner of my eye.

This process repeated for a few nights—a minor annoyance. And then Freckles found his way into the heating vents. You'd hear a "ting, ting, ting" of tiny claws on metal, and Freckles would later turn up who knows where—upstairs, downstairs, every room in the house.

He had the entire system mapped out and became expert at diving for the nearest grate when I was closing in for the capture. It was one of those moments when I made the Grab.

Freckles made the Bite. That thing latched on to the meaty part of my hand between the thumb and index finger and proceeded to bite nearly the entire way through as I ran through the house screaming and shaking my hand. Freckles was latched on like flypaper.

After some reflection, a 9-1-1 call on a gerbil bite just seemed stupid, so I bled a bit, disinfected, washed and wrapped the wound. It healed up nicely.

Thank heavens. I'd hate to break that one out when the guys sit around bragging about their combat scars.

A BOVINE WITH DEATH ON HIS MIND

As I've aged, I've always sort of looked forward to winter. With no yard to mow or weeds to whack, winter generously hands a day of the week back to me, which I spend on enriching pastimes like watching football until my eyeballs roll out of my skull.

It wasn't that way when I was young. For one thing, the current dizzying array of televised sporting events wasn't available in the 1970s. The old cliché is that back then we had three channels. In the mountains, that cliché did not hold. We had one.

The signal from WATE in Knoxville, Tennessee, caromed properly off enough hillsides to be redirected to our antenna eighty feet or so up the hill in our pasture. The quality of the signal varied from pretty good to fuzzy to nonexistent after a snowstorm or lightning strike fried the works.

For years, NBC, and NBC alone, was the network available in the Buchanan household, and it wasn't bad. It offered *Bonanza, Star Trek* and *Daniel Boone*, all of which had better role models than, say, every reality series ever made.

On the downside, my cultural window didn't swing open very wide, which sometimes put me at a disadvantage. At a conference in Raleigh early in my newspapering career—actually it was at a bar, but there was a conference somewhere around there—the colleague I was visiting leapt from his stool like he'd seen Lincoln's ghost.

"It's Charles Kuralt!"

I didn't know Charles Kuralt from Adam's dog. We didn't pick up CBS. My friend turned into a complete fanboy and blubbered his way over to the table of Kuralt and, I think, his business manager. He demanded to buy them a drink and proceeded to swoon and fawn for a while before they made him disengage and sent him back my way.

I couldn't really say I met Charles Kuralt. Although I did when I presented the bar tab those guys ran up to my employer at the time.

Anyway, television was not always the slothful agent it is today, and even if we'd had all the premium sports packages available today, it wouldn't have mattered, because when winter rolled around and hunting season shut down, it was time to turn from the woods to, well, the woods.

We had a nearly vertical chunk of property behind the house that had once been a cornfield but had since become a thriving jungle, and Daddy had his mind set to turn it into a pasture. That involved cutting down trees, clearing brush and burning refuse.

Aside from not being able to watch television, should it be available, Daddy's plan presented one other drawback: Jake. Jake was the first of the annual head of cattle we would raise in the pasture, and he got there before there was much pasture at all. This seemed to put Jake in a dour mood and, being not quite a longhorn but not very far from it, he would attempt to take those moods out on anything available.

At first, Jake took out his dissatisfaction by taking advantage of the terrain and jumping the fence with ease. The fence was plenty high, but it couldn't quite keep up with the slope of the land. Think of it as a high jumper on a track—it's easy to clear six feet when you're already standing at eight feet.

Churning butter was a lot of work, but the effort paid off handsomely. While we had several neighbors with milk cows, Daddy would keep a steer on our steep pasture. Cows in India are sacred because of the Hindu belief in reincarnation. If that's so, it would explain the creature known as Jake—horns and hooves and a half ton of bad attitude, loosed in our field one year. Lizzie Borden had moved on. *Hunter Library, Western Carolina University.*

The solution was to raise the fence to where the pasture resembled the boundary of Stalag 13, and Jake stayed put. And he got surlier. When we went in to drop trees and build and burn brush piles, Jake clearly viewed us as interlopers, and you had to keep an eye on him as he vectored in to defend his turf.

His territoriality wasn't restricted to humans. Rabbits enraged him to no end, and he spent many days digging into our brush piles to flush out the bunny invasion. This backfired on him in spectacular fashion one winter day when we set a brush pile ablaze. It got cooking pretty well when I saw a hare in there working its way out toward the edge. Jake saw it too and immediately set phasers to kill, only Jake didn't bother to go around the bonfire. Figuring a straight line was the most direct path to bunny mayhem, he walked right into the blaze.

Pretty soon, it was evident that Jake was on fire. Just as evident was the fact that Jake flat out did not care. He was dialed in on Thumper with murder in his eyes.

I shoveled snow on his back just as the rabbit broke cover and bolted down the hill. Jake broke as well. It looked a lot like footage from World War II of a Japanese fighter pilot going down and trailing smoke. But this one had a bunny in front of it.

The sight was sort of majestic. I never saw anything like that on NBC.

A BIT OF HORSE SENSE ON THE ECONOMY

The stock market is going up and down like a yo-yo again—more down than up of late—and that brings up a tale of a leading economic indicator: horses, at least one horse in particular.

Daddy was never much for horses. He recounted riding a mule from Tathams Creek to Sylva when he was young and opined a time or two when a mule would be ideal for bear hunting. I think he came to that conclusion after seeing a video of mules taking tourists down the Grand Canyon and reasoned that if a mule wouldn't drop a tourist a mile down into a hole, one wouldn't drop him off a peak in the Nantahala Gorge.

It was a pipe dream he never acted on. I did share his preference for mules over horses. Yes, I know some people love their horses, but I've always been wary of them. My first memory of a horse was attempting to pet a pony a neighbor had purchased for a child. It bit me. For years, I had

Much of Western North Carolina wasn't exactly horse country, gravity being one obvious reason. Daddy considered getting a sure-footed mule to take on bear hunts but never followed up on it. However, several years later, during the Great Recession, I heard a horse tale that was one of the best economics lessons ever passed on to me. *Hunter Library, Western Carolina University.*

no idea the phrase "don't look a gift horse in the mouth" was folksy advice about good manners. I thought it was a warning. You could get your eyes bit off doing that.

But back to economics. In the old days, folks in these parts might have a draft horse for farm labor, but that has gone out of fashion. Today's person who loves horses probably owns horses, houses horses and feeds horses. It is not a cheap undertaking.

Back when the bottom absolutely fell out of the economy, in late 2008 and early 2009, the impact was felt in the equine community, and a lot of people were suddenly facing the stark fact that they simply couldn't afford their horses anymore. A story related to me involves one such gent who came to the conclusion that his beloved steed had to go. Maybe it was more of a nag than a steed now that he thought about it.

He hatched a plan to shed himself of his liability in a humane and forthright manner: He'd get someone else to steal it. At a large horse show in Tennessee, the man pulled up with the loot in his horse trailer. He left it conspicuously unlocked—the perfect crime.

The man went into the show and spent his sweet time roaming around, chatting up folk and basking in the glory of the event. A theme running throughout, it struck him, was that there were an awful lot of people there trying to unload their horses. He got a little worried that no one would steal his offering that evening.

Finally, things wrapped up, and he trudged back to the parking lot. Nervously, he opened the door to his horse trailer and peered in.

Staring back at him was his horse—and three others—gift horses, as it were.

Hope he didn't look them in the mouth.

NOTHING DIVINE ABOUT THIS VINE

It was a summer full of odd jobs, from cleaning restrooms at the Community Service Center to cleaning the trash piled up around dumpsters from people with poor aim and/or discount garbage bags that fell apart at the seams and spread their contents to ripen in the heat, awaiting Jim and his pitchfork.

Those were the pleasant jobs. The unpleasant job was combating the mile-a-minute vine, commonly known as kudzu. Since I was from

Jackson County, I was plenty familiar with kudzu. It was the plant that ate abandoned barns or any unoccupied homestead. It also seemed to have a taste for telephone poles.

We had some county fair prize–winning patches around here—many that really haven't changed over the years, resembling snapshots from the 1960s onward. That puzzled me a bit, as the stuff should've taken over the entire county by now. When I lived in a shack in Cullowhee that bordered a small branch, we had a patch climbing up the bank into the yard and were able to observe that the stuff could grow a foot overnight when the heat and moisture were right. We talked, not entirely jokingly, of shutting the windows at night to avoid being eaten in our sleep.

There was a tale of a group of Cub Scouts whose adult leader was a bit careless in picking a campsite. The group was never heard from again. It's assumed they were entirely consumed. Kudzilla came in the night, leaving only Cubzu behind.

Seriously, the stuff has been recorded to grow up to sixty feet a year. I poked around a bit and found credible sources stating that instead of the millions of acres rumored, kudzu covers only about 227,000 acres and spreads only a couple thousand acres a year.

I'm not sure of the square acreage of the county, but we must have a good chunk of the total acreage of kudzu. I'm not surprised to see the tourism folks promoting that fact. Once you've seen kudzu, you've seen kudzu.

I'd seen kudzu but had the good sense to avoid wading into it, as it was common knowledge among kids that every leaf had a snake hiding under it.

That was until this particular summer, when somebody in power decided to take out the longstanding patch at Mark Watson Park. A gang of us young 'uns were dispatched with scythes to do the dirty work. That work involved wading right into it.

I'd worked some with scythes before but never developed a professional swing. I was as good with a scythe as I am with a golf club—that is to say I swing with a fury, but the results don't match the ambition. My golf shot resembles the knuckleball of the great Braves star Phil Niekro—it bobs, it weaves, it does things a round object shouldn't be capable of.

It made Phil a lot of money, because Phil knew how to make a baseball go over the plate. It's cost me a lot of money because my ball might go over the green or a creek or a four-lane road. On one occasion, I was playing with a foursome on a par-three bordering a highway. The guy playing fourth didn't see me when I winged one across the suicide lane and into a concrete barrier, then ran it down the road with the traffic. Looking at the green and seeing two balls there, he asked me what I hit. I told him a Lincoln Continental.

With the scythe, the swing was just plain dangerous to everyone involved, except the kudzu, so I got tasked to tending to the roots. It was quite an education. I had no idea kudzu roots could run a dozen feet deep—ideal snake den depth, if anyone cared to ask.

All in all, it was a humbling experience because you just knew that if you turned your back on the stuff, in a few weeks it would be back. You can fight nature, but nature is nothing if not persistent, and when it puts its tiny kudzu mind to it, it's going to win.

On the job satisfaction scale, cleaning toilets was a lot more pleasing.

Fresh Fish, Straight from the Box

April is the traditional start of fishing season here in the mountains. It's a chance to dip a line after a long winter off the rivers and creeks. My family participated in that annual ritual, and as a family of outdoorsmen, we enjoyed it, but Daddy decided he'd try a shortcut. He became a trout farmer.

We had a gulch at the edge of the garden with a small branch running through it. The gulch had suffered the same fate as many mountain gulches in previous decades, becoming a dumping ground for old appliances back in the days before landfills and garbage pickup.

Nothing had been dumped in it for probably thirty years before I came on the scene, and most of what had been dumped had deteriorated. What was left was mainly an interesting collection of old bottles that had held concoctions such as liniment and witch hazel and, I would imagine, some stronger stuff here and there.

At any rate, the dump wasn't much of a dump. What trash we did have, we burned in a spot across the branch. Years later at an editorial board meeting where the sins of littering and refuse were being discussed, it occurred to me that maybe we were too poor to have garbage. More likely, the case was, in the words of Cecil Grove of Southwestern Community College fame, "Eat it up. Wear it out. Make do. Or go without." Live like that, and you don't generate much garbage.

Anyway, we had a gulch with a branch running through it just sitting there, and opportunity called.

Daddy's first trout farming experiment was to block the branch and let it fill up in a small pond when hatchlings were deposited. The plan was off to a rousing start until the scent of the fish ran down the branch into East Fork Creek, luring ravenous water snakes from, I'd guess, all the way to the Mississippi. We were overrun, and in short order our trout farm went bust.

Not to be deterred, Daddy, a carpenter by trade, fashioned large fish boxes with metal mesh wire. The mesh was small enough for the fish food to get in but not large enough for the larger water snakes. On a typical day, there would be one or more lying on the screen, eyeballing the trout like a kid with his nose pressed against a department store Christmas display.

So, we were back in business, and the scheme worked surprisingly well. But as these things go, the episode did not pass without a dose of drama—or trauma.

I was in college when the fish farming era was upon us, and in my stint as editor of the student newspaper, I'd often get home barely before dawn. Daddy was a get-up-and-go sort, and these two characteristics met a confluence one morning after he'd gotten up to go to wherever it was he purchased the fish.

I'd been asleep for maybe ten minutes when Mother, who could throw a panic with the best of them when appropriate, was suddenly shaking me, yelling, "THE FISH ARE DYING! THE FISH ARE DYING!"

Daddy had tried to wrestle a fifty-gallon drum full of new trout out of the back of his truck and had tipped it, spilling fish all over the driveway. If you ever get a chance, try going from a dead-to-the-world sleep to scooping up handfuls of wriggling, unhappy fish and sprinting to throw them in the fish box before they asphyxiate in under thirty seconds. It's a sensation I really cannot describe.

Daddy seemed more concerned with trying to not bust a gut laughing than he was with the welfare of his fish—or his youngest son. I'd taken a shower when I'd gotten home and wound up taking my second within half an hour to get the smell of fish panic off before going back to bed.

It occurred to me maybe the whole thing was a dream. When I did go back to sleep, my slumber was filled with visions of goggle-eyed fish staring up from my hands, screaming, "YOUR MOTHER WAS RIGHT! I'M DYING!"

I can't remember why Daddy quit trout farming, but I vaguely recall a cloudburst flushed our little farm into East Fork. I find beauty in cloudbursts to this very day.

THE DARK SAGA OF THE REPUBLICAN BEANS

Turns out, the Republican Beans were an international scandal. Who knew?

I guess I'd better back up a bit here. Jimmy Allman, who recently passed away, was an avid outdoorsman and hunter, which meant he was friends with Daddy. Jimmy was a devoted Republican, and Daddy was a fierce Democrat. Yet the two managed to get along just fine. Yeah, I know, sounds weird to me too when viewed from today's toxic political narrative.

I suppose they just didn't talk about politics but stuck to hunting and, as it turns out, gardening.

There are a lot of great tales about mountain people and their gardens, many that are slipping from memory as the old traditions fall away, such as tales of old men sitting up all night in a patch of woods next to a field with shotgun shells filled with salt to teach a watermelon thief a lesson.

Nobody has time for anything like that these days, thanks, oddly enough, to the devotion we now have to our time-saving technologies. Between email and Facebook and Twitter and Google and the iPhone seemingly welded to the hands of many, we're saving so much time that we hardly have time to do anything else—like have a garden.

You must have skill to have a good garden, but you also must have time—time to plow, time to plant, time to weed, time to check for and deal with bugs and various critters, time to harvest and time to start the whole cycle over.

Before the rise of grocery stores, the garden was a necessity, providing fresh food during the summer and canned and pickled goods to get through the winter. So, mountain folks spent a lot of time with the garden. One of my favorite stories was of Early Deitz, a neighbor of mine who plowed his garden with a mule every year till he was ninety-two. One year Early had crows come in, so he put up a scarecrow. While messing with the garden every day, he also messed with the scarecrow, stuffing its body and legs, putting a hat on it and finally setting it prominently in a lawn chair by his vegetable patch.

Another gent from on up the road, who was quite friendly but also had quite a temper, started going around saying he was going to whup up on Early. Why? "Every time I drive by there, I throw my hand up and the —— never waves!"

Meanwhile, back in our garden, Mother and Daddy grew beans that originated with Jimmy Allman. Although the bulk of their garden was rows of green beans, they loved the bush-style beans. Until the day they died, they called them Republican Beans.

I see Howard Allman on Main Street in Sylva a good bit, and we usually exchange a few stories. Before Jimmy's passing, I'd told Howard about the Republican Beans. After Jimmy's passing, Howard confided in me a tale of a bean scandal.

It turns out we'd been growing outlaw beans the whole time. The U.S. government takes a dim view of certain fruits and vegetables coming across the border, usually with good reason. Like the chestnut blight, snakeheads, kudzu and Asian carp, accidentally introduced invasive species can have disastrous consequences. If you get asked if you're carrying any fruits or veggies when you enter a port to the United States, you can wind up in a little room with very large, very unhappy gentlemen if you answer incorrectly.

Here the story sort of turns from contraband beans to magic beans, and the trail turns cold. The forbidden beans apparently originated in Australia, where a friend of a friend of a friend managed to smuggle them out and into the United States through the ingenious method of putting the beans in his sock.

Needless to say, this was a while back, before you had to take off your shoes for the good folks at security. They didn't cause any kind of a blight but became many a mountaineer's dining delight. I imagine most people knew of the bean's origin. I also imagine Mother, who was a righteous person (not self-righteous; I wish someone would explain the difference to politicians), would have been quite scandalized if she'd known and likely would have pulled them up, roots and all, and turned them over to the proper authorities. I imagine Daddy did know.

Whatever the case, we've got to own up to something, Jackson County: bean bootleggers walk among us.

TURTLES, AND HISTORY, ON THE MOVE

My tortoise was on the move the other day. At any rate, I guess it's a tortoise. I'm no expert, but I gather that the main difference between a turtle and a tortoise is that all turtles are tortoises, but not all tortoises are turtles. Tortoises stick to land, whereas turtles can live on land, in the ocean or in any handy pocket of water. Then again, some land turtles aren't tortoises.

The critter I've seen for the twenty years I've lived at my current location is, I think, a box turtle. As far as I can tell, it moves twice a year—once from a patch of burning bush growing alongside my house down to a patch of juniper below it. A few months later, it moves back. Aside from these moves, the only time I've seen it was when I was burning off and digging up part of that juniper patch. I rescued the tortoise as the flames approached, as it clearly wasn't going to add to its yearly exercise quotient by moving a third time.

The first time I saw this turtle it appeared to be fully grown, so it's at least twenty years old. Looking over turtle literature, there seems to be general agreement that a lifespan of 50 is probably about average, although some may be much older. While poking around, I found one report from 2012 of a turtle in Pennsylvania that might have been 130 years old, as researchers found the year 1878 engraved on its shell.

I haven't heard much about turtle engraving, but I do recall hearing of the practice of people painting the date they discovered a turtle on its shell. We'll stop right here and say it: please do not paint turtles. It's not good for them.

The practice of doing so in the mountains differs greatly from what goes on from time to time in Florida. Remember the local craze from a year or so ago named "WNC Rocks"? People would paint nice messages on rocks and put them around town in easy-to-find spots, hoping to bring a smile to a stranger, who, in turn, would hopefully pass it on.

Florida being Florida, people took to painting turtles in all kinds of elaborate patterns because, well, because Florida is a state where the phrase "geez, tone it down a bit" has never been uttered. It got so out of hand that Florida Fish and Wildlife Conservation issued repeated warnings that advocates of the practice were, in essence, leaving behind beautiful tortoise corpses, as a layer of paint doesn't go well on any living thing. Just look what happened to Tammy Faye Bakker.

Back to the dated turtles: my family was out in the woods so much that it was inevitable that somebody would come across one. This was back in the 1960s, and I vaguely remember the date written on the shell was from the late 1880s or early 1900s. It was a matter of some debate whether the turtle was really that old. Some pointed out that paint couldn't survive on a barn that long, so how could it survive on a turtle?

It was also pointed out that people would lie about the size of a fish or distance of a shot that brought down a deer, so surely some would lie by painting a false date on an innocent turtle. Nonetheless, there was general agreement that in the lore of early mountain settlers, dating a turtle was indeed a practice.

In the end, we decided to treat such dates as legitimate, unless the date ended with "BC." That sort of gives away the game.

This Particular Possum Wasn't Playing

Well, I finally got to hear the story. I've heard it attributed to various tellers of the tale, so I won't credit any one person, though I've heard the late Beloved Man Jerry Wolfe delivered an unparalleled rendition. As I have seen him in action at several events, I don't doubt it. And I wouldn't be surprised if he came up with it.

Anyway, the short version goes like this: "If you're lost in the woods, don't panic, don't run around. Just find you a comfortable log and sit down. Wait for a possum to come by. When the possum moves on, get up and follow him. Possums are experts at getting lost hikers back to civilization. Just follow him. Sooner or later, he'll lead you to a road."

This is one of those stories that has a lot more flavor when heard than when read, but the punchline rings true either way.

When I was younger, I had this theory regarding possums, whose ancestors can be traced back to the time of the dinosaurs. It went along the lines that these critters saw the rise and fall of many creatures great and small—from the T. rex to the passenger pigeon. One day, as a group, they took a look at themselves—rather unattractive, not particularly athletic and their defense is playing dead. I imagine that out of the sheer embarrassment of having outlived worthier species, they decided they'd speed up the whole extinction process by making a date with the interstate.

They're not all innocent victims. I still maintain that some have, well, I don't know what you'd call it, maybe anti-survival instincts.

Back in the 1980s, I lived at a remote end of the Norton community for a while. On my commute, I rarely encountered vehicles, and I'd scan the roadside for the flora and fauna of the season while cruising along. On one such commute, out of the corner of my eye, I saw something on my left speeding down the bank toward the road cut, intersecting with my car. I slammed on the brakes and screeched to a halt just as a possum broke through the ground cover airborne.

It was a remarkable scene, like one of those action movies where the Secret Service agent dives in front of the bullet meant for the president—everything going in slow motion as the agent mouths, "Nooooooooooooooo." It was just like that, only I'd stopped, and the possum missed the grille of my car by a good two yards. He landed with sort of a splat, but I saw him shake it off and scramble out of my vision.

As I leaned out of the window to see which way he was going so as not to squash him, the car gently rocked.

I'd been rammed by a possum. Long story short, he wound up getting under the car, and I think he was heading for the engine in search of possum Valhalla. I shut off the motor, but it still took a stick, some salty language and about ten minutes to get him out.

I was afraid that he might be rabid, but I concluded that he might just be a possum following the possum Prime Directive. The fact is, I like possums. In reality they're generally docile and beneficial—they suck up ticks like vacuum cleaners, and their blood is said to possess immunity properties against snake venom that scientists hope to harness.

But in the end, the evolutionary jig may, indeed, be up. Let's face it, freezing and playing dead are traits that must have worked well for a long time, but they're no match for Henry Ford.

The Fine Art of Mountain Angling

The arrival of warmer weather kind of went in steps back in the day. The garden got plowed, and speculation about when the ramps would hit began. But perhaps the most anticipated step of all was the opening day of fishing season.

Fishing was, thanks to quirks of topography, a very different sport back in the coves than it is generally associated with in the popular imagination. Think fishing, and the images that come to mind are those of kicking back in a boat on a serene lake or the majesty of casting a fly in a graceful arc to a target the size of a quarter. None of that applied in the smaller streams found in these mountains. No, fishing involved bushwhacking your way to a local body of water, rod or cane pole pointed ahead of you to part the brush.

Upon arriving at a stream, one would poke around until finding an opening wide enough to drop a line. If it was warm enough, you'd enter the stream and use the pole to poke overhanging limbs to clear them of water snakes. The shrub was usually so dense that you wouldn't actually see a water snake drop, but you'd hear that distinctive plop of a serpent contacting water. One time I heard seven plops.

I would insert a joke here about walking on water, but I don't want to be sacrilegious. And, to be honest, more straight-up running was involved than walking.

Anyway, if you were lucky, you'd hit something. If you were really lucky, it might even be a fish.

The upper reaches of East Fork Creek. Little mountain streams like these were often teeming with trout. In my experience, they were always teeming with ill-tempered water snakes, or worse. *Courtesy Dave Russell.*

I love just about everything that can be found in water—from scallops to catfish, but I never developed a taste for trout. Deep in the recesses of fuzzy memories I think that may have had something to do with choking on the small bones even a well-filleted trout might have hidden in its recesses.

Like many people, I like lobster, and like many people, I can't afford it. I've read various sources that state lobster was so plentiful in the early days of this republic that it could pile up on beaches, be used as fertilizer and only be fed to prisoners and servants, who sometimes rebelled at the frequency at which it turned up on the menu. I was clearly born in the wrong century.

At any rate, I could catch trout and gut and clean trout, but the trout-savoring gene skipped my generation.

I fished anyway. It was peer pressure—all the cool kids were doing it.

As I was not a skilled fisherman, luck ruled the roost, and I was generally pretty lucky. On opening day, I'd generally yank in a sixteen-inch beauty, creating jealousy among the truly skilled. Things went along like that until a relative tried to teach me how to fish.

See, what I was doing wrong, I was told, was setting the hook too slow. "Gotta snap yer wrist, yank hard."

OK, sure.

Somewhere in Pumpkintown, I applied the lesson with my trusty instructor stationed a few yards behind me. I got a nibble. I yanked and set the hook. And I kept a-yanking, just like I'd been told to do.

From the shallow waters at the end of the line I saw something big—surely it was a legendary trout.

Turns out it was instead the mother of all water snakes. Also turns out that I'd kind of over yanked on my first try. The snake was launching from the creek like it was shot from a catapult. It sailed over my head, and I let loose abruptly enough that the line and pole joined it on its parabola toward my eager instructor.

In the end, it turned out that the hook hadn't set after all, and the snake was soon free-range again. After a week or so, the relative went ahead and got a buzz cut because it was clear that his hair was going to keep standing on end. All the Brylcreem on the planet was not going to change that.

I haven't fished in some years now. As I live near a good fish shop, I do still enjoy the bounty of the seas. Perhaps I can find a way to make that work with my mountain roots. Lobster 'n ramps, perhaps?

SNAKES DON'T TAKE OFF FOR LABOR DAY

In popular culture, Labor Day means the end of summer. It's perfectly obvious to anyone who spends any time outside that there's plenty of summer left, and for whatever reason, the quality of this part of summer gives us yellow jackets and meaner snakes that also know good and well there's plenty of summer left.

So, they're out and up to their snakin' ways.

There really weren't any great snake stories involving Daddy; a chance encounter with a rattlesnake would yield the same results as an encounter with a bear, with the snake on the losing end of the equation.

That said, he didn't go out of his way to kill rattlesnakes. He knew where the dens were and would, on occasion, check on the rattler crop out of curiosity, but he was never one for indiscriminate slaughter.

The snake tale that has hung in family lore involves Mother.

The garden Mother and Daddy raised and tended, often using my brothers and sisters as draftees (me too but to a more limited degree, as my thumb wasn't so much green as bent toward destruction, wittingly or not),

Venomous snakes are part of life in the mountains, the most feared being the timber rattler. Timbers generally stick to a pretty restricted territory but can occasionally throw a curveball. This particular rattlesnake hitched a ride into Walmart in Sylva from Tilley Creek, several miles south. *Courtesy* Sylva Herald, *Quintin Ellison.*

filled the can house shelves with green beans, vegetable soup, potatoes and more. But one treat on the shelves grew wild: blackberries.

The thing about blackberries is that if you have blackberries you have snakes, thanks to one of nature's if/then formulas. If you have blackberries, then you have birds coming in to eat them, and birds are notoriously sloppy eaters. With half-eaten berries littering the ground, mice and rats will follow. And snakes will follow them. I had it rattling around in my young head that snakes liked blackberries before that formula dawned on me.

We'd load up in the truck with empty milk jugs cut off to hold berries and head to places like Bettys Creek, which is developed now, but at the time it was more or less a huge, rambling blackberry patch. Picking the berries was hot, painful work thanks to the blackberry briars. It was also dangerous work at times, thanks to the snakes.

But out of that work, Mother, a wizard of a cook, who could've fed a crowd a memorable meal out of shoe leather—or even a picture of shoe leather—would turn out the best blackberry jelly I will ever consume, along with pies, cobblers, turnovers and more.

You'd always keep your eyes out for snakes while blackberry picking and even more so in places that had the snaky reputation of Bettys Creek. So, it was not without irony that Mother's memorable encounter happened literally a stone's throw from the back-kitchen door.

The garden beyond the back door was a gently sloping affair of about a half acre, but the pasture above it was as close to vertical as they came without being called a cliff. Over the years, it had been used for corn before it went to light forest. Daddy, in one of his enterprising moods, decided to turn it to pasture.

We spent months clearing it, burning the scrub and cutting the locusts into fence stakes to sell for a little extra cash. Over time, we had a couple of hogs and then settled on an annual steer or two. No sooner had we cleared the land than nature, clearly affronted, decided to claim it back. Nature's go-to pitch in the first step of that process tends to be blackberry briars.

So, we had a little patch conveniently located right above the house. One late afternoon, Mother decided to gather a gallon or so of blackberries and climbed the hill, with her feet sheathed not in proper briar gear like boots but instead a pair of worn-out slippers.

Berry picking would commonly go like this: grab the berries on the outer briars, and then pin down the briars with a foot to work your way in to the fruit that was a little better guarded. Mother did this, stepping down on a briar. She apparently missed, and the briar sprang back up. She stepped on it again and again with the same result.

Triple-checking the situation, she discovered that it was not the briar popping back up but a copperhead repeatedly striking, sailing over her slippers—shoes that covered her toes but not the tops of her feet. It was a sizeable snake, and it was just dumb luck that it didn't tag her. Since Mother is a small woman, I do not like to think about how that might have turned out.

Happily, in the end, it was just another family story—one I recall as Labor Day approaches and the heat remains turned up for a few more weeks.

Perhaps until the cold weather sets in, we'll turn to the late comedian W.C. Fields for a piece of advice: "Always carry a flagon of whiskey in case of snakebite...and furthermore, always carry a small snake."

CLOSE ENCOUNTERS OF THE FURRED KIND

Then there was the time I saw an alien. This would have been in November 2013, I think. It might've been 2012.

Either way, I was at Mother and Daddy's on a Friday night after driving straight from work in Asheville. I'd settled in after my routine of making sure medications had been taken and sat in the living room long enough to work up a sweat from the overheated house. So, it was off to the back steps for me. I stepped into the crisp air in the halo of light cast by the yard light out by the driveway. The autumn night was dazzling, and the stars stood out in sharp relief.

This pastoral scene was completely shattered when the alien came staggering around the corner. It had stumpy legs that were only about one-fifth of the length of its body, which was covered in fur. Its arms jutted out at right angles, and where its head should have been, there was only a large tuft of hair. Nothing about this creature added up. The only thing that seemed certain was that it appeared to be hostile.

Being human is a terminal condition, so like everyone else, mortality has crossed my mind from time to time. Disease, nuclear war and car wrecks were some of the things I figured could be the end of the line for a certain boy from East Fork. A demonic interstellar Kewpie doll? I did not see that coming.

All in all, considering the complete lack of philosophical preparation, I was handling the scene with stoicism and grace, right up until the moment it marched in front of me and turned slightly in the glow of the yard light.

This was not a hostile alien at all. This was a skunk.

It was doing something I'd never seen a skunk do—walking on its front legs. And that tuft of hair where the face should have been wasn't a tuft of hair but the locked-and-loaded weaponry of a skunk aiming to settle some scores. It was aiming right at you-know-who.

Somewhere right along in there, the flop sweat started flying. I wanted to bolt so fast that you'd have to FedEx my shadow to me. But the critter had the drop on me. I considered raising my hands in surrender but figured staying motionless was best. It worked. Skunks have lousy eyesight but hear well and have a good sense of smell. (There's a joke there somewhere.)

I reckon it could smell the fear and hear my teeth chattering. Or maybe it just got tired of doing a handstand. Whatever the case, it dropped to all fours and moseyed off.

When I was young and would go coon hunting with Daddy, the dogs would sometimes get after a skunk. Back in those days, a lot of the old-timers' homes near creeks were on stilts, so you could walk or crawl underneath with ease. My instructions were simple: do not let the dogs run a skunk under a house, where a fight could break out and serious spraying would commence.

I never got sprayed during those encounters. I've never been sprayed in my life, even in these later years. That's just dumb luck. Like many mountain natives, I once possessed superb night vision, but staring at computer and phone screens all day for decades has wiped that out. Thanks to this, I've had a few encounters, such as when I pulled a Mr. Magoo and was reaching down to pet the skunk between my feet before I realized it wasn't the cat.

And I guess I was really lucky I didn't get sprayed at Mother and Daddy's. There were skunks all over the place—they reproduce very efficiently—and it was not uncommon to find two or three running patrol in the wee hours. They'd just appear out of nowhere, like they'd been beamed down from the starship *Enterprise* or something. We never figured out where they were coming from.

But it turns out they were living under the house. Fortunately, by that time, Daddy had run out of dogs.

MORE SNAKES COME OUT OF THE WOODWORK

There was a fair amount of snake lore that involved the old-timers; one particularly unsettling example was of the newlywed couple who started a fire in the fireplace on their first night in a mountain cabin only to warm up and awaken the den of rattlers that led to their demise later that night. I heard that story enough that I suspect there was some truth behind it.

There was a tale Daddy would tell about a circuit-riding preacher who ventured into the backwoods of Little Canada. Coming upon a cabin perched on a rock outcrop, the preacher was greeted by the young lad of the house, who was home alone while the parents were out and about on some chore. The youngster invited the preacher in to wait for his folks, and the usual awkward silence between elder and youth quickly set in.

Looking for an icebreaker, the child asked the preacher if he'd like to hear some sangin'. Not expecting much from a youth who'd certainly received no choral training, but perhaps hoping he'd stumbled upon a natural, the preacher politely said sure, he'd like to hear some sangin'.

So, the kid picked up a piece of cordwood stacked by the fireplace and gave the cabin's clapboard wall a good hard rap.

Sangin' ensued from who knows how many rattlesnakes.

I'm not sure if that preacher saved anybody that day, but he evidently wasted no time saving his own hide by mounting up and heading out of there.

Brother-in-law Boyd Ensley (*left*), Daddy (*right*) and a couple of other mountain natives, albeit recently deceased. *Author's Collection.*

My former Asheville coworker Russ Williams related a story about when he and a date were out in rural Alabama and stopped at an overgrown roadside picnic table to have a bite and rest. They were beset by a sizeable rattlesnake, an eastern diamondback, I imagine. The snake treed them. Atop the picnic table and weighing their options, they saw a pickup truck pull off the road. The driver assessed the situation, reached into the bed of the vehicle and retrieved a golf club.

Wading into the weeds, he took a swing and sent the snake's head and body off in opposite directions. Then he chucked the club in the back of the truck and went on his way.

Russ's companion said, "That fellow must be one heck of a golfer."

Russ responded, "Probably not, if he's that used to playing out of the rough."

One of my favorite snake stories was one I heard not in the mountains but on a golf trip to Florida. My late father-in-law, Joe Pristas, was an avid golfer and belonged to a swanky country club. He'd take me in tow on early morning outings.

Given my upbringing, the club itself wasn't particularly my cup of tea, but the crowd Joe hung with was, like Joe himself, people who had succeeded in life despite growing up in the hardscrabble echoes of the Great Depression.

One friend of Joe's was a Texan whose name escapes me, but he had a good story that I'll never forget. Growing up dirt poor on the Gulf Coast, he and his friend spent time trying to figure out how to make an extra dime. A lot of those plans involved a posh resort in the area, one that featured a swank French restaurant.

One day while lollygagging in the dunes, the two came across a pair of sizeable rattlesnakes that they promptly dispatched. They figured the serpents had to be worth something to someone, and after studying the matter for a while, the two arrived at the conclusion that if the French ate frogs and snails, surely rattlesnake had to be on the menu as well.

So, the duo found themselves sauntering through the dining room of the restaurant, shouting for the cook while patrons of fine dining turned their attention away from their plates to address how best to climb the walls. Not wanting the place to be cleared of customers and staff, the chef came through the swinging door to the kitchen and purchased the snakes to be rid of his unwanted vendors.

Through the swinging doors, they clearly saw him step out of the back of the restaurant and unceremoniously deposit the snakes in a garbage can.

If I recall correctly, they sold the guy the same snakes three times before he caught on.

3

Mountain Character,
Mountain Characters

TECHNOLOGY UNWINDS SOME OLD TRADITIONS OF WATCH POCKETS AND POCKET WATCHES

I was rummaging around in one of our trinket baskets one day and came across a pocket watch and a Rolex. There was a time when pocket watches were a sort of a marker in the lives of mountain men. They were a sign of maturity and stability. A great deal of courtliness centered on pulling the watch from the watch pocket, flipping the cover, checking the time and carefully replacing the watch in the pocket, making sure the watch chain didn't tangle in the process.

These days, I'm not even sure if they make pants or suits with watch pockets or pocket watches, come to think of it.

Watches were once rather fascinating things full of gears and cogs and whatnot. Most folks around here relied on their Timex watches. They were built well, well enough that John Cameron Swazye ran out of ideas on how to break them in a series of commercials advertising their ruggedness. He ran over them with snowplows. He strapped them to various vehicles. He made them watch the *Jerry Springer Show*. Nothing could deter them.

You bought a Timex, you wound it and you expected it to accurately tell the time for years. If the watch did eventually break, there were places that repaired watches. If it was broken so badly that there was little hope of getting it fixed, you handed it over to the children. I recall attempting to fix watches—all the kids in the neighborhood would often help.

None of us ever actually fixed a watch. We'd unpack the guts and gingerly try to coax life back into a deceased Timex. When that failed, we'd try to repack the guts, and it was always like trying to put ten gallons into a five-gallon hat. Still, the attempt would be time well spent on a lazy summer afternoon.

Then, one day, someone handed me a broken watch; I cracked open the back and all that was staring back were circuit boards.

My watch-fixing days were over. The same phenomena killed my nascent career as a mechanic when I popped the hood of my truck back in the 1990s, ready to prime the carburetor with some gas, and I couldn't find the wingnut to open up the carburetor or the carburetor itself. For all I know my current vehicle has a basket of hamsters under the hood.

It reminds me of a line the great newspaper columnist Richard Reeves once related: "I've survived through several recessions and downturns, particularly after I got my degree in mechanical engineering from Stevens Institute of Technology and soon found out that Texas Instruments was selling everything I knew for about $20."

Technology can be cruel.

I guess I'd better explain about the Rolex before I wrap up. It was about as fake as fake can be. A friend had been on a trip to Southeast Asia and brought back a whole bag of them. Still, I would wear it to postdeadline, predawn poker games with a group of sports writers I once hung out with, just to let them know I'd be able to cover whatever sort of crazy bet crossed my mind. If that didn't work, I figured I could toss it behind me when they were chasing me out of the game. One of them would surely make a grab for it and slow the others down.

The sad part is, it was probably still the most expensive watch I've ever owned.

GRANNY WAS UP TO SNUFF WHEN IT CAME TO BEE STINGS

A couple of coworkers were discussing wild mushrooms one day. These folks know what's what in the fungi world and had been consuming that year's crop with great gusto. I stay away from mushrooms in the wild because I assume that they're all deadly poisonous. I only eat the ones I buy in the store.

I base this on the theory that grocers know killing off their own customers is a lousy business plan—the success of the cigarette industry notwithstanding.

Anyway, the mushroom talk got me to thinking about snuffboxes. No, not the snuffboxes associated with elderly women of these mountains but the devil's snuffbox, a fungus that can be found in these mountains.

Also called puffballs, snuffboxes were a delight to find because you could stomp on them and get a satisfying explosion of spores like a bomb going off, except your foot would still be intact.

As the purpose of the snuffbox is to propagate itself, I don't think they took any offense to this practice. Then again, I did read that inhaling those spores can cause a lung disease called lycoperdonosis, so maybe I'm wrong about that. For what it's worth, lycoperdonosis comes from the genus name for snuffboxes, *Lycoperdon*. This translates to, um, a wolf passing gas. Never let it be said that botanists don't have a sense of humor.

As for the other snuffboxes and the elderly mountain women who dabbled in dipping, Grandmother Buchanan was one of them.

Her place on Tathams Creek was the gathering spot for cousins, where we'd generally spend time tearing up the woods or running around barefoot in the yard. There weren't snuffboxes in the yard, but there were quite often copperheads, and we ran up a streak of several years where a barefoot cousin would step on or over one of the critters. The law of dumb luck prevailed, and no one was bitten.

Grandma imbibed. It was a pretty common habit not long ago, and I'll be danged if I can figure out how it evolved. I'd like to say, given that dipping seems to be fairly confined to areas like this one that are heavily populated with Scots-Irish, that it came over from Scotland, but given that tobacco was a New World crop, that would be impossible.

For whatever reason, women in Appalachia and surrounding regions took to dipping back in the eighteenth century. Some were pipe smokers as well. I found an account written by Vicki Betts that recounted a Yankee captain in Alabama calling on a home with three young women, saying, "Each of them had a quid of tobacco in her cheek about the size of my stone inkstand, and if they didn't make the extract fly worse than I ever saw in any country grocery, shoot me."

I don't recall Grandma spitting, but she did enjoy her snuff. It was probably Dental Scotch snuff, a popular brand.

Looking back, the trend does puzzle me, particularly considering that the vast majority of mountain women I noticed dipping were generally paragons of virtue. I guess, looking back, the habit appears pretty ridiculous, kind of

Grandma Buchanan lived well into her nineties and just got feistier as she got older. A dedication to snuff may have kept her going along the way. *Author's collection.*

like how forty years from now people will wonder what caused the Great Belt Shortage that led to young men walking around with shorts around their knees and their underwear hanging out.

Dipping did have one bonus for the flock of kids running around in Grandma's yard. Inevitably, one of us would careen into a yellow jacket's nest, and after being lit up, would be instructed to shut up, quit crying and go see Granny. She'd rub some of that dip saliva on the sting, and the results were like witchcraft—instantaneous relief. Sure, naysayers point out that putting human bacteria, not to mention a poisonous plant, on a wound isn't exactly hygienic, but after a sting I'd just ask, "Where's Granny?"

Given the encounters with the copperheads, I sometimes wondered if that cure would work on a snakebite as well. I'm glad I never had a chance to find out.

HUMOR GENE CAME FROM SOME SPECIAL LADIES

Mother's Day is a time to appreciate those who raised and mentored us. It's a time to appreciate the mothers still with us and to appreciate what carries on in us from mothers since departed.

In my case, Mother instilled a gentleness and sense of forgiveness that I have found invaluable over the years. I was always amazed at how she would not speak ill of anyone, even if it was well documented that they deserved it. I was always in awe of how she put others first. And I'm thankful I inherited her love of humor—a trait that ran even stronger in Grandmother Deitz.

I was a wee lad when Grandma passed, but I remember her fondly and have been told by several people that I inherited her sense of humor—an ability to laugh at pretty much anything. That's a dandy trait to have these days. Have you seen the news lately? Go look. I'll wait.

Pretty loopy out there, right? In recent months, I've lost track of the number of times someone has talked to me about a particular news story regarding current events and ending with, "It just seems crazy to me." I generally respond that it doesn't seem crazy. It flat-out *is* crazy.

The final resting place of Ransom Vanderbilt Deitz and Mamie Deitz, my grandparents. Mamie died when I was young, but I've always been told she was where I got my sense of humor. Ransom died before I was born, and the theory holds that he was given the middle name Vanderbilt in hopes that he'd be as rich as Cornelius Vanderbilt. It didn't work. *Courtesy Dave Russell.*

So, a sense of absurdity is a nice thing to have. But it can be perilous out there in the adult world of fantasy make-believe.

I'm talking the world of Corporate America. During my years in Corporate America, I saw a lot of silly things. You can start with the fact that a CEO makes about a zillion times more than a typical corporate drone who actually, y'know, works. My rule of thumb was that when someone was on vacation and I couldn't tell because my workload didn't increase, they probably weren't serving much of a function in the first place.

The silliest stuff, in general, involved the corporate training sessions. We had training on leadership. There was some merit in that session, in that you could tell when someone was trying to pull some leadership on you. We had training on this and that. Some was useful. Some was clearly just so the corporation wouldn't be sued for this or that because, hey, we'd had training not to do that, right?

We had one session on how to sit in a chair. It was difficult, but I eventually mastered it. I'm even sitting as I write this today.

The training that nearly sank me was sensitivity training. It was the early 1990s, and special attention was being paid on how to not offend anyone.

A large number of us were gathered in a room where we listened to solemn speeches about the evils of insensitivity. After the windup, we were presented with the "money shot," a vivid example of real-life insensitivity in action.

It was a clip from *The Simpsons*. Having worked nights for years, I'd never seen an episode, or even a clip, of *The Simpsons*. As we all sat there soaking up the insensitivity of the particular skit that was supposed to send us to our respective fainting couches, a thought occurred to me. "This," the little voice in my head said, "may be the funniest thing I have ever seen." The voice added, "We may be in real trouble here."

I bit my lip. I held my breath. Tears were beginning to trail down my cheeks.

Then it happened. I snorted—repeatedly and really loudly. The humor of the skit and the absurdity of a bunch of grownups who couldn't laugh at a cartoon, well, it all sort of came crashing down and totally smashed the vibe of the workshop.

People gave me that cold stare that said, "This guy is clearly not getting with the program." Fortunately, the event wrapped up, and I think the organizers were too embarrassed to try to pull off another one.

I'm not insensitive. But I did pick up from Mother and Grandma the common sense to, when you see something funny, go ahead and laugh. My supervisor didn't see it that way and had a talk with me. That brought out something I didn't get from Mother: my temper.

Not sure who I got that from.

HILLBILLY UPBRINGING HAS ITS PITFALLS: AN INADVERTENT LESSON IN SENSITIVITY TRAINING

I would not trade being raised in these mountains for anything. My upbringing was during a time when the land was still largely unfettered and easy to explore—the people bound by decades of history. But as I was to learn later in life, that upbringing was not entirely free of pitfalls.

You see, in many ways, folks were closer to life back in those days, when it was not uncommon for a mountaineer to hit the door and spend most of the day outdoors interacting with the forces of nature. Maybe because of that element, while folks were closer to life, they were also closer to death. It was not uncommon for a son or daughter of these hills to have known someone who died in a logging accident or farm accident

Daddy during his stint in the navy during World War II. Although he was a mechanic stationed stateside at a naval flight base, he saw an awful lot of death as the United States rushed planes and pilots out the door to deal with the Axis threat. A familiarity with death, though not of the human sort, was something I was exposed to in an early life hunting and fishing and was something I became perhaps hardened to. It almost cut short my career in the newspaper business, as it turns out. *Author's collection.*

or the multitude of diseases we've largely put back in the box thanks to modern vaccines.

On top of that, I grew up around a generation that, if not headed to or returning to Southeast Asia, had become all too familiar with the war through Korea or World War II. Daddy never served overseas, but he was a mechanic stationed at a naval aviation training base in Florida. He never talked too much about that, but later in life, he did let on that while he was there, thirty-two or thirty-six—it wasn't a number he was eager to closely track—people lost their lives in training accidents.

And beyond that, the closeness to nature and death was a given. People had to eat, and instead of going to a grocery store, that food was in the pasture or henhouse. Farm to table was a lot more personal than looking at an expiration date on a shrink-wrapped package.

The folks I grew up around were not a squeamish lot. If you hunted or fished or had a farm, you were familiar with death as part of life. Some of that rubbed off on me. And it bit me in the rear a few years back in a nearly career-ending episode.

So, I'm working the Sunday night rotation to put out the Monday morning paper, and there's little news and absolutely no art for the front page. I searched through the news wires, growing increasingly desperate, when, ah, there it was.

Across several time zones, in Honolulu, an elephant performing with Circus International had become enraged and critically trampled her groomer before killing her trainer and breaking free. Police chased the animal through the city streets, firing dozens of rounds before bringing the animal down. The photos were, I thought, the closest things I'd ever see to Godzilla loose on the streets of an American city.

I picked one for the front page.

Meanwhile, over in our printing plant, another native hillbilly, a friend of mine not long out of the marines, was setting up the page for printing. I can only imagine his thought process when he must've looked over at the red ink and decided he'd do me a favor to get the colors to pop a bit so readers could better see what was going on in that picture.

There was a time around here when in your youth you would hunt, and every now and then that hunt would come to a logical and messy end. There was a time when that sort of activity was just as natural a part of life as could be. I'm not sure when that time was over, but it was evidently over before publication of that particular edition.

About one hundred calls came into the newsroom and eventually several dozen letters. Some of the politer ones suggested I be flogged.

Well, a couple of weeks dragged on, and the commotion finally died down. I was driving home from work when I topped a hill and found myself looking up at a large billboard advertising the paper. That front page was on it.

The corporate marketing folks upstream had apparently managed to not read our little publication for the entirety of two weeks. And off to the races the whole affair went once again.

I've had a lot of nicknames over the years. "The Elephant Man" was probably my least favorite. And I still won't respond to a marketing survey to this day.

AT ONE LOGGING CAMP, A NEAR-FATAL DOSE OF GRAVY

Mother could cook. Man, she could cook. I recall one time after a hunt when Daddy and I, with my buddy Geoff Cantrell in tow, returned to the house for a meal. Mother loved to feed people. Geoff loved to eat, though he never seemed to gain a pound. It was a match made in heaven.

There's a famous scene in the movie *Close Encounters of the Third Kind* in which Richard Dreyfuss more or less loses his mind and constructs a model of Devils Tower National Monument out of mashed potatoes. Geoff pretty much replicated the scene, except Dreyfuss doesn't actually eat the Devil's Tower in the movie.*

Like most mountain women, Mother made a few precious ingredients go a long way and unfailingly put out a good spread, particularly for the first meal of the day. I think we were a bit different than many families in that Mother had a good touch with oatmeal, but she also had a good touch with a mountain mainstay: sawmill gravy.

Not everyone had such a gifted touch. Daddy told a story about sawmill gravy almost getting someone killed. In the early 1900s, it was said that a squirrel could jump a chestnut tree in Maine and go all the way to Georgia without touching a different species of tree or the ground. At about the same time, the chestnut tree blight appeared, and by 1940, it had virtually eradicated the chestnut forests—perhaps four billion trees.

Chestnut trees were big—four feet around at the trunk and one hundred feet or so tall and were often straight and branch-free for the first fifty feet. And they could stand for decades after dying. Thus after the first wave of

Blackwood Lumber Company built a mill town at East LaPorte in Jackson County. It included a standard-gauge railroad from Sylva to East LaPorte. Such mill towns became small communities, sometimes complete with families, schools, churches and baptisms. Farther back in the mountains were rough camps restricted to only rough men. From such a camp came a tale of sawmill gravy in quantities that very nearly led to murder. *Hunter Library, Western Carolina University.*

This page: The Blackwood train. *Hunter Library, Western Carolina University.*.

Lumber camps provided riches from the earth, stacked in the background, and were often also the scene of spiritual celebrations. *Hunter Library, Western Carolina University.*

logging of virgin timber in these mountains, there was another wave devoted to taking down "acid wood," the gigantic chestnut ghosts.

Some of the acid wood logging camps had one hundred men or more, and they had to have something to eat. More often than not, that something was sawmill gravy. In some places, it was more often than more often than not. It was every meal.

Now, sawmill gravy can vary. Sometimes it's made with bacon drippings and cornmeal, sometimes with sausage drippings and cornmeal and sometimes with sausage crumbles added in. It is usually finished off by adding milk, diluted milk or just water. It was referred to in some cases as "life everlasting," as it gave the men energy and kept them alive.

The name "sawmill," however, evidently started with accusations that even the cornmeal was being skipped, and people were eating acid wood shavings. (For a bit more on the topic, I recommend Joseph Earl Dabney's *Smokehouse Ham, Spoon Bread, & Scuppernong Wine: The Folklore and Art of Appalachian Cooking*. It is a good cookbook but also one of the best Appalachian history and culture books I've read.)

So, a friend of Daddy's was in this particular camp, and they were being served sawmill gravy for every meal, and it wasn't going over very well with a gentleman from Madison County. He threatened both the foreman and cook with unpleasantness if the menu did not start to vary immediately.

Another meal rolled around, and another row of plates of sawmill gravy were presented at the long dining table.

Mr. Madison was not happy. As Daddy recalled, his friend "was a little slip of a feller and needed the food, and he could see what was about to happen, so he grabbed his plate and put it behind his back."

The irate logger jumped on the table and proceeded to walk down its length, kicking one plate after another off while seasoning the air with some creative language. And off to the foreman's tent he went.

"I want my pay," he said.

"Payday ain't till Friday," the foreman responded.

"I'm from Madison County," the man said while drawing a pair of pistols (they looked like cannons, Daddy said) and laying them on the boss's desk, "and I'll be paid."

And son of a gun—no pun intended—he was paid. The foreman seemed to be glad to be shed of him. The cook, as I recall, may have reconsidered the merits of being a one-trick pony.

Mother could cook sawmill gravy. Some people can't. If you can't, watch out. Turns out bad sawmill gravy might be bad for your health—life threatening, even.

Mr. Cantrell has taken pains to point out that his Devils Tower was smothered in gravy.

Explosive Tales and a One-of-a-Kind Hobby

So, there's this joke going around: a young man receives a call from an elder who needs help with his roof. The guy's ninety-four years old, so the youngster figures he can go out to the man's house and take his sweet time on the roof doing repairs unmolested. But when he shows up, the man is running up and down a ladder to the roof, carrying bundles of shingles and working frantically.

The worker asks the old man what's up—how he's so limber and energetic at that age. "Well, I'll tell you," the man says. "Every morning at breakfast, no matter what you're having—biscuits, eggs, fruit, whatever—take a little gunpowder and sprinkle it on. Not much, just a few grains. Do that and you'll see results."

The young man figured the guy was pulling his leg but got to thinking on the matter and out of curiosity did as he'd been advised. As the small amount of gunpowder was undetectable and didn't alter the taste of anything, he kept it up for a week or so and soon just got into the habit of it.

Time went by, and he noticed that he quit having allergies in spring, never got the flu in winter and in general never had any health complaints. So, he kept it up. And it continued to work.

The young man eventually turned into an old man himself and stayed hale and hearty until death came for him in the form of a motorcycle wreck at the age of 102. He left behind eight kids, twenty-three grandkids, seventeen great-grandkids and a thirty-foot crater where the crematorium once stood.

I told that joke to Howard Allman as he was taking his daily walk down Main Street one day. Howard said he'd heard stories of people slipping gunpowder into the feed of a plug horse to make it act livelier when attempting to sell it. Is that true? I don't know. I do recall that Ichabod Crane's horse in Sleepy Hollow was named Gunpowder, so maybe that's a reference.

I have seen stories of people using gunpowder as a food seasoning back in the nineteenth century. Gunpowder back then was more or less a combination of charcoal, sulfur and potassium nitrate, so maybe that's possible. I certainly don't recommend it, and I really don't recommend using modern smokeless powder, most of which contains nitrocellulose. If you ate a bunch of that stuff and had a bout of gas, I imagine your remains might end up in low Earth orbit.

I got to thinking about powder and blasting a bit after a visit to my mother-in-law. She related a story about a hobby she had in her youth that definitely would have made her a prize winner on the old *What's My Line?* game show.

Powder blows things up, and in war, it also blows people up. A lot of those people survive traumatic injuries and go on with their lives. Such was the case when Beverly, my mother-in-law, was looking for something to do to help kill time when her husband, Joe, was off at military training. She became the scorekeeper for a one-legged bowling team.

This was back in the days before advanced prosthetics, so the bowlers would hop up to the line on one leg and toss the ball. It was apparently quite a challenge, as the team of veterans generally had a grander time accusing each other of fouls for being over the line than any serious attempt to roll a good frame.

LEARNING TO DRIVE INVOLVED MOMENTS OF SHEER TERROR

One thing I'm glad I never experienced is a school lockdown drill—or a real lockdown, for that matter. Safety must not have been a concern back when I was in high school, as I don't recall anyone being seriously injured in a violent incident. On the flip side, very few of my classmates seemed very interested in safety.

As I recall, they quit having fire drills there for a while. See, the evacuation zone was the school parking lot. The school parking lot was full of cars. Cars could be used as a means of transportation to, say, drive to the lake and go for a swim. As such, only about half the student body came back from a drill.

The funny thing is, in those days, the majority of the pickups in the school lot had a rifle hanging on a rack. They weren't considered threats because they weren't used as threats. It was a different world.

That's not to say schools in the 1950s, '60s and '70s were entirely devoid of terror. There was one source that still makes my hair stand on end when I think of it today. Ladies and gentlemen let us discuss driver's education films.

Mechanized Death.

Highway of Agony.

Wheels of Tragedy.

For four decades or so, titles like those—yes, they're real—would appear on a blackboard or projection screen once the lights went down and the clackety-clack of the film projector fired up. The acting was bad, the narration was preachy and the lessons offered were simply common

The path of US 441 over Cowee Mountain. Yes, there's a road there somewhere. If mountain roads weren't scary enough, driver's education was scarier still, involving tales and films of the carnage-filled commutes ahead. *Courtesy* Sylva Herald.

sense—don't drink and drive, don't speed, don't be reckless. And remember that the guy in the other car may be reckless, drunk, speeding or just plain stupid. Fine. Check.

But the wrecks—lawsy. There were missing legs, missing heads, bodies cut in half, bodies missing half a head and burned bodies. And it was footage of real people in real wrecks. Some kids would throw up, some would faint dead away—and those were the football players. Some of the more sensitive souls would simply bolt from the room. Some of them can probably still be found out there in the woods today, curled into the fetal position deep in the underbrush.

I'm still surprised that entire generations didn't swear off driving after being exposed to that stuff. Of course, we now live in an age where children are raised marinated in media. Not so long ago, the public school might be the first place a youngster was exposed to any kind of visual stimulation. You never knew how they'd react.

I recall a story of a mountain first grader who was being raised in an isolated cove and got his first experience with the visual arts. It was a filmstrip version of "The Three Little Pigs." Filmstrips were essentially a series of slides projected one after another and were sometimes synched up with a soundtrack on a tape player. They were cheap, durable and could provide a quick lesson. On the flip side, they were handy for killing some time when the teacher didn't have his or her fastball working on a given day.

So, this mountain kid—I picture him in my mind barefoot and in overalls—saw his first filmstrip, and he was absolutely mesmerized with the timeless tale and bright colors. He was really smitten and completely into the experience, leaning in wide-eyed to soak in the tale. When the pig's house of straw was blown down by the Big Bad Wolf, he gasped audibly, still rapt. When the pig's house of sticks was blown down, well, the kid was onto the game and didn't like where it was headed one bit.

He leaped up and shouted, "Why that son of a ——."

I'm pretty sure that was the end of the filmstrip for that young lad. I wonder if he ever heard how the story turned out.

Itching for a Visit from an Old Nemesis

It occurred to me one day that Daddy was onto something. This wasn't because of something that happened but because of something that didn't.

For the first time in just over twenty years, I found myself in the middle of winter without a case of poison ivy.

Now, breaking out in poison ivy when it's twenty degrees outside seems odd, but it can happen a few different ways. With its identifying leaves gone, it can be mistaken for more benign vines, so it's understandable that folks grab it while doing a little off-season landscaping work. The stuff can also be found on firewood, and you can get a dose hauling it in and burning it.

I've heard tales of schoolyard bullies back in the old days stuffing vines down the pants of a hapless target, causing breakouts to the point that parents had to stuff the victim in a bath of oatmeal to ease the itchy torment. Fortunately, I don't recall hearing of that sort of cruelty around here. Vegetative mayhem tended to run along the lines of stuffing a teacher's desk drawer with ramps. I guess people were just more refined in these parts.

At any rate, I picked up annual cold weather ivy from another source: our cat, Butterscotch. Scotchie was an indoor/outdoor cat of the scattershot variety. Once out, she wanted in; once in, she wanted out. Mostly, she just wanted her way. In the winter, that way involved going out, finding a patch of poison ivy, rolling luxuriantly in it and returning to my lap to lacquer me with ivy juice. This went on for years—she lived to be older than twenty—before I figured out why I was breaking out with ivy rash in the middle of winter.

On one of the nature shows past the news channels on cable television was a documentary detailing how certain species of birds rile up spraying ants. They get the stuff on their wings, and it helps kill parasites or something, if I recall correctly. I did a little research to see if poison ivy helped cats in some manner. The research showed no such connection. The conclusion of my research, instead, told me something I'd known for years: my cat was a jerk. She was intentionally swabbing me with resin.

I say "was" because, after surviving five or so presidential terms, Crystal Pepsi and Roseanne Barr's rendition of the national anthem, she shuffled off this mortal coil in 2017. She took her chemical warfare patrols to kitty heaven.

If I'd followed Daddy's credo, I could've avoided it in the first place. He had a firm rule: no animals in the house. They stayed outside. Inside was for people. Further, he expected animals to have utility. Cattle were for meat, barn cats were for catching mice and Plott hounds were for catching bears.

Daddy loved his dogs, but when it came to animals, he had one rule: inside the house was for people only. That rule was broken one time and one time only, and the results were truly spectacular. *Author's collection.*

The one time that Daddy's rule was broken, it was broken in spectacular fashion. One of Mother's sisters was visiting from out of state, and along for the ride was the family poodle, as nonutilitarian a dog as Daddy could ever imagine. We all headed out to visit some folks at the head of East Fork, and somehow or another, Daddy was conned into letting them leave the dog in the house.

During the trip up the creek, one of those sudden mountain storms brewed, bringing torrents of rain and the sort of intense thunder old folks used to describe as the mountain dwarves bowling back in the hollows. We wrapped up the visit and went home.

When we got there, about three shelves up on the cupboard beside the kitchen table stood the poodle—in a puddle of its own making.

I don't believe a person's head could actually explode, but behind Daddy's eyes were what appeared to be miniature nukes going off. He looked toward the poodle puddle, back toward Mother and then toward my aunt, trying to process the scene. Off in the distance I swear I could hear the sort of music that fills the air when a matador steps into a bull ring. He was clearly ready to break every rule in the ASPCA handbook.

"This is gonna be some vet bill," I thought to myself.

I looked at Daddy and reconsidered.

"Mortician bill."

Somehow, and I'll never know how, he composed himself, and carnage did not occur. But that was the last animal, save a mouse, inside the house on East Fork.

If I'd followed that model, I could have enjoyed many rash-free winters. With Butterscotch gone, that winter marked my first one rash-free since Bill Clinton was in office.

I'm just glad we didn't live near a nuclear waste dump. I hate to think what would've happened if she'd had access to the high-test stuff.

A TIME WHEN PHONES WERE A PARTY

A video circulated on YouTube showing a group of young 'uns—the current generation that has technical prowess unmatched in human history when it comes to communications technology—attempting to use a rotary phone. Needless to say, they failed. Oh, they figured out how to dial, but they didn't figure out that you had to take the receiver off the cradle first.

The video brought smiles to the faces of graybeards everywhere. Of course, if you sat any of us wise old heads down at a telegraph, we'd have no idea what to do. Such as it is with communications technology; you stay up-to-date, or you get left behind.

I recall when Daddy learned how to use the phone or, to be precise, how to use a rotary phone. I imagine he knew how to use its predecessor, the crank phone. At any rate, he didn't come to this skill late in life because he was slow, but it was because he'd never really had to use it before. One day it dawned on him that it would be a useful tool for his passion and avocation—bear hunting.

I suppose prior to the phone, he'd simply planned what pass to head to in the predawn hours by talking to work buddies who hunted with him or in passing conversation while waiting for Mother to emerge from the supermarket. I reckon that he'd headed off to Caney Fork one time too many when everyone else headed to the Nantahala Gorge and set out to remedy the situation.

And learn a rotary phone he did. He also learned a pitfall of phone service in the area—the party line. Party lines would serve up to ten households, which created a few obvious drawbacks. For one, the line could be tied up for hours on end; if somebody else was on, you couldn't call. There was also a complete lack of privacy. Some people just loved to eavesdrop. Of course, if you were on the line, you could detect a telltale click when someone else picked up. At times, you could hear muted breathing. At such times, some kids would start lying like dogs, laying out elaborate fictitious plans to rob a bank or three over the weekend. You could hear the pace of the breathing of the eavesdropper pick up.

None of this mattered to Daddy. All that mattered was that someone was in his way while he was planning a hunt, and he was not a patient man regarding such things. I don't vividly recall him telling someone to get off the —— offline. But then again, I wouldn't swear that I didn't.

It didn't take him long to master the rotary phone, but I do confess that I enjoyed watching the process. That's because Daddy had this fuzzy concept that a person should emerge into this world knowing certain things, like how to run a chainsaw or fix a flat, without it ever occurring to him that such things, in fact, had to be taught. Well, he had to be taught how to use a phone.

I'll confess I'm not a great adapter to new technology. My wife fought me for years over getting a cellphone, saying I needed it for safety if I had a breakdown. I told her to buy me a gun, reasoning that it would keep me safe and I could attract a wrecker with a couple of signal shots, but she finally won out.

The manual for it was thicker than the one for my car. Daddy never got a cellphone and often lamented people walking around in a daze, affixed on their own palms. Daddy was onto something, I think.

PATCHING TOGETHER A LOOK AT SOME FASHION NO-NOS

I suppose making fun of fashion has been in fashion as long as fashion itself has, well, been in fashion. Who am I to buck the trend?

On every college or public school campus I've been on recently, a new fashion trend is in evidence—threadbare jeans. These are jeans that, as the name implies, are worn down to the point that the flesh is exposed, generally at the knees but sometimes all up and down the legs. At times, there is more flesh than thread in evidence.

One can only assume good money was paid to attain this look. My first reaction upon seeing them, however, was how Mother would have reacted.

"Those children," she would have thought, "must be so poor. They can't even afford patches."

Patches were once standard-issue fare for jeans in the mountains. You'd rip a knee out playing football or whatever and a patch would be applied.

Unpatched jeans were a rarity. Patches got extra mileage out of jeans. Mountain women took great pride in their patching skills, which they developed over years of crafting patchwork quilts.

Of course, applying patches to today's threadbare jeans would leave you with more patch than jean. Then again, who knows? That could be the next fashion trend. And it's also rather practical, as patches generally seemed sturdier than the surrounding jeans.

At any rate, jeans have been the paramount fashion trend of my life. In the '50s, it was jeans with T-shirts; in the '60s, it was jeans with no shirts; in the '70s, it was bellbottom jeans; in the '80s, it was jeans with a sports coat; and onward it's been jeans with a sports coat and tennis shoes instead of dress shoes.

Look at photos prior to the '50s, and you'll notice a couple of trends. Men wore hats—Stetsons or fedoras—and they also wore ties. I mean, all the time. In one of Bob Plott's tomes on hunting in the Smokies, there's a photo of a group of bear hunters after a successful day in the woods, lined up with their kill. One of them is wearing a tie. He might have been wearing a tie in the event that he lost his dog leash. Maybe that strip of cloth around his neck was fated as a backup. I can't imagine any other reason to be wearing a tie on a bear hunt. I'm just not sure who you're hoping to impress. Your Plott hound? The bear?

Daddy sure never wore a tie in the woods. Quite often, he was wearing barely anything after tearing through a laurel thicket, but Mother would patch up his clothes, and he'd jump right back in.

I cannot think of a more useless piece of clothing than a tie. There's zero utility in a tie. It does not hold your shirt on or your pants up. Speaking of holding your pants up, fashion is quirky. It can also be straight-up vicious. The height of fashion one day is going to look ridiculous in twenty years. The shoulder padding women sported in the '80s looks goofy today, as do the aforementioned bellbottoms of the '70s.

But it takes a special kind of ridiculous to look goofy from the get-go, which brings us to sagging jeans. The ban on belts in prisons is supposedly what gifted us with this trend—a trend strong enough that the culture as a whole started putting up signs banning people showing more underwear than jeans from establishments.

Again, this is a special look that has the added punch of having zero utility. A friend of mine in Henderson County had a chain-link fence around her yard, and one day a gent with no belt was fleeing the authorities when he tried to hurdle it. The sagging jeans grabbed the links as he went over, pulling his pants all the way down and leaving him upside-down and completely trussed up. He'd still be dangling off that fence today if my friend hadn't seen him swinging in the breeze.

Of course, if Mother had witnessed this, she would have expressed sympathy. So poor that he couldn't afford a belt.

When Disaster Strikes, Sometimes It's Best To Not Pick Up the Phone

The noise coming from the phone sounded for all the world like a swarm of angry bees. Geoff had another live one on the line. Florence came, hitting our Eastern North Carolina brethren hard. It will go down in the books as a storm that others are measured against. It proved a minor inconvenience here but was a life-changing event for a lot of folks.

It won't be a measuring stick here in the mountains. We'll keep remembering the twin storms of 2004, the floods of 1940 and 1916 and the blizzard of '93.

Natural disasters bring out the best in some people. They bring out the worst in some people. And they bring out the weird in some people. And when the weird got going, they called Geoff Cantrell.

I've been fortunate to have Geoff, who now works in the public relations office at Western Carolina University, intersect my life repeatedly. He grew up on Balsam, the son of a park ranger. Our joke was that his daddy chased my daddy, which wasn't always entirely a joke. We went to high school together, worked at a weekly newspaper together for a couple of years and later at a daily for a decade or so.

Geoff is as nice of a guy as you'll ever meet, but he possesses this odd quality. The eccentric are drawn to him like moth to a flame. The blizzard of 1993 produced a bumper crop.

I didn't have much in the way of a crisis with the two-plus feet of snow we were smacked with that year. I did have to run my sister-in-law to the ER the night before the flakes began piling up thanks to a bout of food poisoning from a now long-defunct restaurant, but I had her back at the house before the roads began closing. We never lost power.

After a few days, I-26 and I-40 reopened, and I was ready to go to work. My sister-in-law, having been stuck for four days, was ready to head back to Ohio. I dug her van out, moved it so I could get out and began the commute to work, which took about three hours even though it was only twenty-five miles or so. (Everyone got back on the road at the same time, and it didn't work well.)

I got out at the job site, reached into my pocket and had a sinking feeling when I realized I'd driven off with my sister-in-law's keys. So, she was stuck with us for five days.

Anyway, we all had it better than Geoff, who was stuck at work with no food but a vending machine. It was around this period that he started getting the oddball phone calls. Once he was on the line for a half hour or so. All I picked up from the conversation were the usual Geoff-isms: "My goodness," "Well isn't that something," that sort of stuff.

When he hung up and turned to me, I couldn't describe the look on his face. "Bewilderment" will have to do. "That was my Aunt Gladys in Chattanooga," he said.

"How is she?" I asked.

"I don't have an Aunt Gladys in Chattanooga."

During disaster, tempers run high as patience runs out, and that brings us back to the call that opened this chapter. The phone rang, and Geoff picked it up. (Fun fact: Back at the weekly, I barred him from answering the phone on Thursdays, the day the paper came out.)

"Bzzz. Bzzz bzzz bzzz."

"Yes sir, I understand, but—"

"Bzzz bzzz BZZZ bzzz."

"Yes sir. But this is the newspaper. We don't have anything to do with that."

"BZZZ BZZZ BZZZ!! (click)"

"So, what was that all about?" I asked.

"Guy wanted his power back on. I told him we didn't have anything to do with that."

"What was that yelling at the end?"

"He yelled, 'That's the same thing the sheriff's office told me!'"

Maybe It's Time to Bring Graft Back

Roadside springs were once a thing here in the mountains. You might be in the middle of nowhere or you might be on a busy four-lane road when you notice a pipe sticking out of a bank with water gushing out.

Mountain springs were famed for providing a refreshing, cool drink year-round. *Hunter Library, Western Carolina University.*

It seems kind of alien these days, but it was there for the taking. There was one spring on Cowee Mountain that almost always had a car or two parked by it with people, jugs in hand, filling up. I drank from it a time or two, and it was fine water. I imagine some of the people slaking their thirst were tourists who were parched from hours on the road. But I also recognized local folks filled up an empty milk jug or two.

It turns out that cool, clear liquid wasn't restricted to water in the mountains. This photo, which is believed to have been taken around 1967, includes (*from left*) Guy Sutton; Fred Holcombe, who was Jackson County's sheriff from 1962 through 1986; and Holmes Allison in front of the old jail with a confiscated moonshine still. *Courtesy* Sylva Herald.

I got to thinking about spring water when, of all things, I was perusing an article about campaign spending. The incident that came to mind was many, many years ago, when I saw a local politician approach a fellow whose land I was helping clear at the time. The politician handed the gent a pint of what appeared to be spring water, they shook hands and the politician moved on to his next call.

Now, as there was a tasty spring piping out not one hundred yards from where this transaction went down, and a pint of spring water wouldn't go very far on such a hot day, I was perplexed. Was "gifting" water some new fad? Was the canning jar a keepsake or something?

And then it hit me—that wasn't spring water in the jar at all. That there was something else entirely. That was what made Popcorn Sutton famous. More to the point, that was campaign spending a few decades ago.

There's always a time in the cycle when the glossy fliers start arriving in the mail, saying a person you thought was OK or probably haven't spent time thinking about at all is a scourge on the Republic—someone who, if elected, will surely bring pestilence and plague o'er the land.

It's little wonder people get so upset during elections and before and after. A good bit of the time, you can't even tell who's behind the junk filling up your mailbox. A lot of time, if you can run down the source—something that's getting harder to do all the time—it turns out the mailing comes from some faraway person or organization that likely couldn't tell the difference between Tuckaseigee and Turtle Wax.

So, I have a proposal. In the interest of keeping us all sane, I say instead of people with too much money and time on their hands hiring consultants to figure out which politicians they can buy and then hiring more consultants to design ads to make us upset, angry and frightened enough to head to the polls, let's cut out the middleman (or men, or women).

For every $10,000 donated to pay down the national debt, give those people one extra vote and take away their ability to fund candidates or ad campaigns. Hear me out—I see a few advantages here.

For one, if Daddy Warbucks parts with a million or a billion dollars here or there, he'll have plenty of extra votes, possibly enough to sway a county or perhaps state judicial election. However, the damage would be localized. Instead of somebody helicoptering in and showering bucks on a lunatic candidate running in a distant state, they'd only be soiling their own bed by casting extra votes for their own lunatics.

Secondly, you'd be able to watch a ballgame, turn on the radio or walk back from the mailbox in peace.

And the debt could disappear overnight.

Now, such blatant graft might remind some folks of the bad old days. But it seems healthier to me. Sure, there was always a chance that the intended voter might go blind if the candidate happened on a bad batch of, um, spring water. But honestly, even a pint of poisonous get out the vote was probably less toxic than what we're being exposed to these days.

Love of Sports Veered into Dangerous Territory

ACC basketball nearly gave me frostbite. Let me back up a bit.

You find a lot of odd things roaming the woods while hunting. One might come across a collapsing barbed-wire fence in a dense forest with no sign that a pasture had ever been anywhere near or that cattle had evolved, for that matter.

On occasion, I'd come across wires strung from tree to tree, placed about as high up as a man could reach or climb, spaghetti-ing along for hundreds of yards and in some case miles. One day I got tired of climbing a mountain to see where the thing terminated and turned downhill to see where it might have been coming from. After a bit, I hit a stretch where someone had obviously pulled down some of the wire, but just as obviously (cue scary music), it was coming from my own house.

At some point, Daddy had evidently lugged a television antenna to the top of the mountain. For the young 'uns, here's a bit of history—there was a time not all that long ago when there was no cable or satellite television available in these parts. That meant you had to pluck a television signal out of the air using an antenna. In flat parts of the world, you could simply put the thing on your roof. Here in the mountains, with signals from far-flung cities bouncing around willy-nilly off ridges, that usually didn't work.

That meant lugging an antenna up the mountain, wires dangling, and hoping things would stay connected and you'd wander into a broadcast hot spot. There, if you were lucky, you'd plant the antenna like the marines planted the flag on Iwo Jima. If not, you got to climb a tree and somehow connect the thing in a manner where it hopefully wouldn't be taken down by the next high wind.

Given the weather here, the shelf life of a TV antenna was around six months. They were lousy at pulling in a signal but were great as lightning rods. By the mid-'70s, we had quite an array around the house that had given their lives to treat us to *Bonanza* and *Star Trek*. Our steep pasture sort of looked like something the military had put up to detect approaching German bombers. It also looked like the bombers had won, with bits and pieces of technology dangling from poplar trees following lightning strikes. Oh, and if you did get a signal and wanted to change the channel, you had to get up and do it manually. They were barbaric times. (Caveat: We didn't have to get up to change the channel at our house because we only got one.)

Television meant sports, and sports were about as good as it got back in the 1970s. The basketball squads of Duke, NC State, UNC and Wake Forest would gather early in the season to play one another in a tournament called the Big Four, with the two winners of the first round playing for the title and the two losers playing for third.

"Big Four" sounds kind of conceited, especially to the other ACC members, but the fact is that those four schools won sixteen of the first seventeen league titles and twenty-seven of the first thirty. Big Four games didn't count in league standings, but they set anticipation for later games that did.

One year when we were again between functioning antennas, the tournament was coming on, and I was tasked with wandering around trying to find a signal so we could watch Wake Forest and UNC duke it out. As luck would have it, the signal was coming in right behind the kitchen window. As luck wouldn't have it, there was no place to secure the antenna, so I wound up standing in the backyard propping the thing up during the game. As a courtesy, the TV was moved to the kitchen table so I could watch.

Did I mention it was snowing? Because, yeah, it was snowing. Between the snow on the screen and the snow building up on my eyebrows, I had a hard time telling who was winning, but it must have been a good game because nobody ever did see if I wanted to come inside.

SIGNS OF THE (FORGOTTEN) TIMES

There was a brief trend a few years back where grocery stores put advertising on their floors. It was mighty unsettling. For one, even though the ads were printed on the floor, they looked like something loose that you could slip on. Also, so many products are branded with human beings—fake or real—that you were inevitably going to wind up stepping on, say, Betty Crocker's face while reaching for the V8.

Advertising folks are creative, and there's no end to where they can wind up slapping an ad. But for my money, examples of true creativity can be found by winding the clock back half a century or so. Those examples could be found on the winding backroads of these mountains and the rural South.

Friends, meet Burma-Shave and Rock City. Burma-Shave was introduced in 1925 as a liniment that didn't sell all that well. Looking for something that would, Burma-Shave brushless shaving cream hit the market, backed by a clever advertising campaign. In 1926, using a series of small signs spaced out along America's two-lane roads, the Burma-Shave jingle started its march toward fame.

There were usually about six signs spaced out and offering a rhyme that ended with the final sign boosting Burma-Shave. Early on, most were conventional ad pitches, but as the campaign evolved, there were signs to boost the war effort in the 1940s and quite a host of highway safety messages, such as the following:

Drowsy
Just remember, pard
That marble slab
Is doggone
Hard

He lit a match
To check gas tank
That's why
They call him
Skinless Frank

If daisies
Are your
Favorite flower
Keep pushin' up those
Miles-per-hour

On curves ahead
Remember, sonny
That rabbit's foot
Didn't save
The bunny

These signs could usually be found a few feet off the road. A bit farther off the road was the rise of "See Rock City." Beginning in 1935, Rock City founder Garnet Carter hatched the idea of offering to paint barns along thoroughfares for free to advertise his attraction near Chattanooga, Tennessee. He further enticed farmers with free passes or promotional items, such as Rock City thermometers. He was said to offer as much as three dollars to diehard holdouts.

I've been to Rock City, but I never actually saw it, as the day we were there it was socked in by a fog so thick you couldn't see your hand in front of your face. For all I know I might have been standing in the middle of a soybean field. We didn't pay to go in because we couldn't find where you paid to go in. I'm just happy I didn't drive off the mountain on the way up or down.

Anyway, Carter got a gentleman named Clark Byers to do the painting, and he converted around nine hundred barns in nineteen states before he decided to hang it up in 1969, after nearly being hit by lightning for the umpteenth time.

As for Burma-Shave, it peaked at around seven thousand signs in forty-five states. The Rock City campaign ended with roadside beautification laws and a painter who didn't want to experience some of the more esoteric laws of thermodynamics. Burma-Shave went the way of the dodo when traffic moved to the interstates, where cars moved along too fast to read that sort of ad campaign.

The sign campaign ended in 1963, but sentinels of the times could be seen standing along roadsides for years. Over time, errant drivers or, eventually, the weather, which also wore down many a Rock City barn, took them down.

A Cool Mountain Spot When the Heat Is On

Some years back, I got involved in a minor controversy regarding the South. It was an author, as an endless array of authors seemed to be doing at the time, opining about what a swell town Asheville was. The new had worn off of that topic for me, but I was game and agreed to be interviewed.

The conversation ground to an abrupt halt when he started going on about what made Asheville such a charming southern town. I pointed out that it wasn't a southern town. It was a mountain town. There's a difference. I won't go into history. I will go into simple geography.

With summer barely underway in June 2018, the thermometer stood at ninety degrees in Sylva. I checked the temperature in Columbia, South Carolina; Tuscaloosa, Alabama; Memphis, Tennessee; and Raleigh and came up with ninety-five, ninety-five, ninety-four and ninety-five. And the heat didn't appear to be backing off anytime soon. This was just as we started taking the wrapper off summer.

The difference between the mountains and the South is that here you can still find a semblance of relief from the heat when it's summer. Go to Deep Creek, and you'll hear the squeals of people from a hundred yards off as they jump into water coming off the heights of the Great Smokies. I learned at an early age that wasn't the case once you came down off the mountains in the summer. You can cut the atmosphere with a knife. The water is listless and lifeless. Of course, there is life, but it's mostly in the form of cottonmouths and alligators.

Off the mountain, that's when you're in the South. People died down there in the days before air conditioning. Mountain folk had their own air conditioning, though it's become little but a yard decoration these days. I'm talking about the springhouse.

In search of a homestead, water was the foremost concern, and a mountain spring was a prized find. Once located, a structure was thrown over it to keep it clear of debris and critters. A lot of times, this started as a

Former police chief George Evans (*left*) is shown with Burt Wilkey and a cache of illicit alcohol. Moonshine that wasn't destined for sale or trade often wound up stashed in a nearby springhouse, where it was kept cool and doled out by the men when prying eyes weren't around. *Courtesy Sylva Herald.*

small log building, but over the years, it dawned on most people that wood that is constantly wet is wood that's going to rot, so the log buildings turned into stone structures.

Stone holds cold well, and as a result, a springhouse was a place for a cool drink of water even on the hottest day. Springhouses were used to store meat and produce that would otherwise rapidly spoil. Since they were sort of secretive buildings usually off by themselves and with only one entrance, I suspect they often stored illicit substances of the day that were best kept away from prying eyes. Yeah, I'm talking moonshine.

Due to their construction, springhouses were often the last structures standing after a farm had been abandoned. You can still stumble across springhouses, or the signs, in remote areas that are now federal land—the site of onetime homesteads otherwise reclaimed by nature. In some places, the springhouse, the chimney and maybe a stubborn patch of forsythia are the only telltale signs of someone's home.

Of course, all is not romance regarding springhouses. I vividly recall helping clean out a springhouse I'd been slaking my thirst from for years. With the cap off, my cousins, who had also been drinking from it for years, and I were treated to the sight of a good half-dozen salamanders swimming around in our drinking water.

The old-timer on hand put our shock in perspective: "They're alive, ain't they? That's good water." I'm pretty sure that's a phrase you only hear in the mountains. In the South, there might have been an alligator in there. Alive would be a bad thing, I reckon.

Sharp Edges and Dull Minds

Mountain people have frugality embedded in their DNA. I suppose that's a good thing, because most mountain people had little to rely on other than the land on which they lived. "Land rich, dirt poor" is the operative phrase. As such, when Daddy passed away in 2015, a year after Mother passed in 2014, there was little in the way of earthly possessions to be parceled out as a way of preserving their memories.

The items we had, though, were meaningful: a set of well-seasoned cast-iron skillets; some oddities, like a Ziploc bag containing several rattlesnake rattles from snakes Daddy had dispatched over the years during his jaunts in the mountains; and the topic of this chapter, a number of pocketknives.

These were carefully doled out among family members. Like most people growing up back in the day, Daddy carried a pocketknife from the time he started wearing pants. They were always razor-sharp, thanks to the family whetrock.

That was another family heirloom. Whetrocks (I always pronounced it "whitrock"), or whetstones, water stones, oil stones or simply sharpening stones, were valued tools. Years back, they were prized possessions—naturally occurring stones found only in a select number of mines. Japan and Belgium were renowned for the stones, although these were mined in the United States as well. As with many items, they've been replaced with manufactured stones.

Regardless, the whetrock at our house was well worn because it was used religiously. Pocketknives, kitchen knives, scissors, anything with an edge was given a workout, and any edge in the house would cut you if you weren't careful.

Pocketknives were valued commodities, and knife-trading was a popular pastime. Mostly, though, folks here would hang on to a knife. Pocketknives were used to whittle, to dig out briars from the flesh or to double as a screwdriver in a pinch. This was before mass-produced knives flooded the market and before mass-marketing pushed those knives on the public via infomercials.

I must admit, the pitchmen in those commercials were quite skilled. I found myself watching one as I was unwinding after a late night at work. They had a special that night—three hundred knives and maybe a sword or two, plus the "But wait! There's more!" I already had a knife. But I had to admit the commercial left me thinking maybe I could use three hundred more.

The habit of carrying a knife is hard to shake, and I still carry a multi-tool everywhere I go. It doesn't come in handy very often, but when it does,

Back in the day, everyone had a pocketknife. Some were used for skinning squirrels or gutting fish; some were used for whittling, and pretty much all were used for comparing and trading. In one case, a pocketknife was used in a breaking and entering—a case an enterprising peace officer cracked in an ingenious manner. *Hunter Library, Western Carolina University.*

there's no substitute. This habit was developed before the era of infomercials. It was also developed before the era of metal detectors, and that led to me being involved in some very uncomfortable conversations in courthouses and airports.

A coworker of mine—for the sake of argument, let's call him Dave Russell—was in a major airport about to depart for a week's vacation when it dawned on him that he was carrying a multi-tool. He stuck it in a potted plant, and it was still there a week later when he returned.

One of my favorite mountain knife stories is one I heard at an old gas station/store in the Cashiers area. This was thirty years or so ago, and the proprietor related an incident from at least thirty years prior to that, when he'd been the victim of a breaking and entering and had a quantity of merchandise disappear. The sheriff at the time—I don't recall his name—searched the scene and found the broken-off tip of a knife that had been used to pry open a window lock. The sheriff pocketed it.

A couple of weeks later, some local boys came in for conversation around the pot-bellied stove; one of them seemed to jump a little when he saw the sheriff in the corner. The sheriff concocted a reason he needed a pocketknife and put on a great show, patting his pockets and puzzling about where he'd left his. He asked the young man if he might borrow his blade. The young man complied. The sheriff opened the knife and pulled out the broken tip from his pocket.

If I recall the story correctly, the crime was solved, and the criminal was arrested on the spot. That was some sharp detective work.

Maybe We Should Tackle Litter Differently

Sometimes the Better Angels of Our Nature Just Don't Show Up

I've spent a lot of time recently thinking trashy thoughts. With all the litter cleanups around here—desperately needed and most welcome—it's been hard not to.

I hear a lot of talk about how some people need to change their habits, quit littering, et cetera. That's true. But is it doable? People get stuck in their ways, whether those ways are admirable or not.

I say we attack the problem from other angles. Anyone who grew up in the latter half of the last century probably remembers bottle deposits. Back

A photo of ancestors so old that we couldn't find anyone left alive who could identify them. While the family is obviously not wealthy, one thing that strikes me about the scene around the weather-challenged home is the lack of trash. My theory is that in the era of "land-rich, dirt poor," folks couldn't afford trash. Everything was reused until it was used up. *Author's collection.*

before plastic overran the globe, drinks came in glass bottles. You could turn those bottles in for a couple of cents or a nickel each.

On any given Saturday, kids and some adults would fan out and clean the ditches along area roads. There were times when it was actually difficult to find trash. You wouldn't get much money, but it would be enough for a candy bar and a soda, and that would be enough incentive. Apparently, we need some kind of incentive once again because the amount of trash out there is incomprehensible.

It's obvious that 90 percent of the stuff is tossed from vehicles or blown from the beds of trucks. Why this is, again, I don't know. We all gas up, so just toss your trash in the garbage can at the gas station, or the garbage can at the grocery store, or the garbage can on Main Street. Really, they're everywhere. I've seen pictures.

But it seems that garbage cans are invisible to a subset of humanity. The military spends billions of dollars a year on research to make planes and tanks and troops invisible to the enemy. Maybe they should just dress a military unit or two in garbage cans because there are evidently a lot of people out there who they could then sneak up on.

Anyway, I think we ought to abolish plastic bottles and probably plastic shopping bags, which my friend Dave Russell refers to as "urban tumbleweeds." We got along without them for thousands of years. We'll adjust. Plastic bottles, in my view, are one of the biggest scams ever perpetuated on humanity. This goes back to the days when every community had a good, easily accessible public water system. You drank that water from a glass or a hose or the pump that you cranked to draw it from the ground. Then the plastic bottle came along, and suddenly, that water costs as much as a soda once did. It's just water. Coincidentally, there seemed, just as suddenly, to be a shortage of drinking fountains.

I think if you went back in time seventy years and told an old-timer that you were paying for water—and radio, television and a small fortune for your phone—they probably would have put you down on the spot. Out of pity, mind you, as someone who would pay for what should be free is surely the kind of simpleton who would be falling down an open manhole cover soon enough, so why put first responders through all the bother of recovering the body?

Some years back, I read an entertaining blog post from a fellow—let's call him Kevin for the purposes of this story—who drank his morning coffee in Styrofoam cups. He got to thinking about how those cups never break down and how they'd still be around in landfills many years from now, waiting for alien archaeologists to unearth. So, he started writing his name on the cups, thinking they'd find so many that they would think he must have been some kind of king or demigod. Kevin could be found everywhere—his name left in permanence for future scientists to ponder his awesomeness.

Then he got to thinking about it some more, and it occurred to him those alien scientists would eventually figure out that all of Kevin's trash had helped wreck the planet and led to the extinction of Kevin's species. They would think Kevin was a monster—a selfish monster, one who had thoughtlessly wrecked his own civilization.

So, he started writing his ex-wife's name instead. Oh, well.

It's heartening to see the kind of cleanup efforts we have around here sometimes. I just wish it wasn't so much work to stay ahead of the Kevins of the world. Taking that coffee cup away from him in the first place might be a start.

A WINNER IN THE "SWEEP" STAKES

Daddy was good with a broom, though not as good as Mother—she could spot individual dirt atoms. And he was not as good as the old generation of mountain women who would sweep their barren yards and somehow make that dirt look clean. But he was good in the way carpenters have to be good at clearing sawdust out of worksites. He didn't so much sweep the sawdust as hurl it—a flick of the wrist that launched a cloud of debris out of the way.

I thought of that when I was sweeping out our mud room a couple of weeks ago. It reminded me of a story a Jackson County native told me some years back. I'm not going to mention the gent's name, as we lost track of each other a few years back, and I'm afraid he's gone on to his eternal reward. But I would hate to declare him gone if that's not the case.

This fellow told stories about how you need to remove a certain gland from a groundhog before cooking it, was a firm believer that there are mountain lions in the area and was a devotee of old-time gospel singing. He'd been around a bit in his life, and he shared a story of the most successful sweeper.

Like many here, this Jackson boy went off to seek his fortunes after World War II, when the country's economy kicked into hyperdrive. He wound up in or near Atlanta, working for a company that churned out quality hardwood flooring. I gather this was sort of tongue-and-groove flooring—the type that snaps together. As he told it, the quality was particularly high and it was in great demand both from contractors and do-it-yourselfers, and the plant was running nonstop.

The trimming process for the flooring was pretty precise, but this was back in the days before computers figured everything out, and because of the high volume of production, there was a good deal of scrap. There got to be so much that the firm hired an elderly man to sweep it up for twenty-five cents an hour. In pre–air-conditioning days, I suspect that it was hard, sweaty work.

At any rate, the man did his duty for a few weeks and then approached the suits who ran the place with a proposal: he'd sweep for free if they let him keep the scrap. As it was just being hauled off to the landfill or burned, it likely sounded like a great proposal. It's also likely that they questioned the man's sanity.

Fast-forward about a year, and the man had his own crew working for him, driving a dump truck to haul off the scrap. The man had hung up his broom and was riding around in a suit, driving a Cadillac. That's what happens when you corner the market on supplying quality hardwood chips to every barbecue joint in the greater Atlanta area.

4
Moving through the Year

REWARDS OF RAIL-SPLITTING WERE ELUSIVE

The interlude between the end of hunting season and the start of growing season for the Buchanan household on East Fork usually featured a project or two. The project usually involved clearing a plot of pastureland, but sometimes it might be more ambitious, like the Saturday morning when I was awakened by a crash and saw one of my favored uncle's legs dangling from the ceiling.

As I observed blue sky through the gap of the struggling appendages, I surmised something was missing. That would be the roof. The old tin roof apparently had sort of needed replacing. Now it was gone. Therefore, it now definitely needed replacing.

Fortunately, before yanking it off like a bad toupee, Daddy had rounded up a crew—he'd helped a lot of people put up their own homes—and before nightfall, the new cover was in place. I rarely got the memo on such projects.

This was the setting when it dawned on Daddy that instead of just clearing land for pasture by downing, piling and burning trees and brush, there was a profit to be had. We'd cleared our way to a stand of locusts. It was my introduction to rail-splitting.

Locust makes an ideal fence rail. You cut a downed tree to uniform lengths, limb it and get a couple of wedges and a sledgehammer. Perhaps notching the tree with an axe first, you drive home a wedge to split the

The split rail fence is as emblematic an image of the southern Highlands as there is. Daddy and I cut locust rails over several winters, and I was frequently reminded that Abraham Lincoln was famed for his rail-splitting, the lesson being that perhaps it would help me build character just like Honest Abe. Years later, I'm still waiting for it to kick in. *Hunter Library, Western Carolina University.*

tree lengthwise—perhaps using a second wedge inserted into the initial split—then finish the job with an axe or crowbar if that is called for.

Speaking of wedges, one of Daddy's phrases was "cold as a wedge." Now, we were splitting our rails in winter, and wedges are made of metal, so naturally, they were cold. But so was everything else. I couldn't divine any particularly heightened coldness in a wedge. When someone had a nasty blow to the head and was knocked unconscious, Daddy would amend the phrase to "knocked cold as a wedge." For some reason, I always thought that sort of made more sense.

Anyway, I didn't really take to rail-splitting, but we did OK, selling them for, I think, seventy-five cents apiece at a feed 'n seed, and Daddy would give me a cut. For quite a few Saturdays, we'd be out there downing and dragging and wedging and stacking, and it occurred to me that I was experiencing a historical kinship with none other than Abraham Lincoln, Rail-Splitter.

The tale was that Lincoln split rails. This developed character. Lincoln had oodles of character. He had spare character lying around all over the place. He had character to the point that, later on in life, he went about emancipating people.

A Saturday would come and go, and another Saturday would arrive. We kept splitting rails. I kept building character. But instead of building a desire to emancipate, I only built a desire to be the emancipate-tee. I figured I must've been holding my mouth wrong or something. At any rate, the trees kept coming down, and the rails kept going out until the glorious day when rail-splitting came to an end. We ran out of locust trees. But Daddy had saved enough for posts to fence in the freshly cleared pasture.

I was like a kid shaking out a Cracker Jack box with no prize inside. I could hear fate cackling over my shoulder: "No emancipation for you, bub!" Clearly, I had been had. That said, in retrospect I soon learned that splitting rails beats digging postholes in earth that appeared to be 80 percent rock by a country mile.

Also, it didn't seem to be very good at building character. Maybe that's why you don't hear tales of Abraham Lincoln, Post Hole–Digger.

Going Batty Over a Burst of Wild Onions

Wild onions appear in force as one of the first harbingers of spring. Years ago, my in-laws were on the porch with Mother and Daddy discussing various gardening topics, when the conversation settled on the stinky little things. The in-laws had lived on a dairy farm at one point early in their marriage and never forgot how the Holsteins got into a patch of the stuff, which rendered their milk sour and undrinkable for days.

It's a shame people can't eat them because they sure are prolific. Actually, I have eaten them or, more accurately, inhaled them by accident while mowing or weeding. I spent most of my formative years on my bicycle or friends' motorcycles, so I've inadvertently swallowed just about everything that can become airborne. Stinkbugs are the worst.

Perhaps the one airborne critter I thankfully never inhaled were bats. This brings to mind a couple of stories.

When I was six or so, one of my brothers and I were walking down East Fork after dark, when a one-in-a-million event occurred. A bat chasing a bug I had neglected to swallow dove at my feet as I walked, and I found myself standing—one foot on each wing—with the little fellow pinned. So, I reached down and picked him up—one hand per wing. I couldn't wait to get home, as I was sure Mother would be delighted with my catch.

Now, I've been wrong about things in my life. Thought Carter would beat Reagan. Thought we would've had flying cars by the time I was thirty. But I'm not sure I've ever been more wrong than when I anticipated the delight in Mother's eyes when I brought home a cute little bat. I got to the front door, kicked on it and held the little feller up. The door opened. There was a silence as a palpable lack of delight settled over the scene. Mother never cursed, but in that moment, it appeared she might be reconsidering that stance.

She looked at me, looked at the bat and a torrent of panicked verse began to issue forth. She was going so fast that I couldn't catch much of it, but I could tell about every third word was "rabies." I was clearly faced with a conundrum. Should I turn the wing held by my right hand loose, I would be bitten on the left and get rabies and vice versa.

Shooed away from the porch, I moved out into the yard and threw the bat up two-handed, much in the form of a bride tossing the bouquet. To this day, I think of bats at weddings. It beats thinking of divorce, I suppose.

Speaking of weddings, my wife had a bat entangle itself in her hair back in high school and has a tendency to head for the hills every time she spots one. It has made fireworks viewing and drive-in theaters something of a challenge.

My fascination with bats continued long after I bagged one. On early spring evenings, a favorite activity was heading to the cemetery at East Fork, picking up some pea gravel and lobbing them toward the twirling bug-eaters. They'd usually catch a few of them. After a bit, they'd catch on to the game and start dive-bombing us with our own rocks.

One time, out of curiosity, I spent a few minutes tossing up green onions. No bat ever grabbed a one. I reckon that makes them smarter than dairy cows.

PLOWING TIME

From Tractor to Tiller to Mule

As the ground slowly warms, the smell of freshly turned earth begins to waft over the mountains. It's hard to describe—a mix of the smell you get when earthworms surface after a rain and of, well, life lying dormant ready for another season. Turning the soil is a long tradition in the mountains and a necessary one for many families who are heavily dependent on subsistence farming to provide fresh produce for both the long and short haul. The family garden is sort of going by the wayside, but they're still out there in spots. Thus the soil is still being turned, and to turn a garden of any size, you need a tractor.

Pulling that off in the mountains takes skill. After one of Daddy's heart attacks, he asked the doctor if it was OK if he continued walking. The doctor agreed, recommended it, in fact, but only on level ground. To which Daddy replied, "I ain't got no level ground!" Mind you, I know good and well Daddy was already thinking about getting back out in the woods to bear hunt and was going to do so regardless of doctor's orders. He wasn't asking for permission. I'm not sure why he asked at all, outside of some sort of theoretical curiosity.

At any rate, Daddy was right about the lack of level ground. You could drop a golf ball on just about all of the property and watch it merrily bounce away toward the creek. The five or so acres on East Fork was nearly all uphill or, if you turned around, downhill, and that included the garden.

Grover Cabe and later his son, Andrew, would come break the soil every spring with a tractor, and it was pretty impressive to watch. It's easy to understand why you hear about tractor and riding mower accidents here in the hills. Gravity doesn't fool around. Breaking the garden with a tractor is a graceful thing to watch, but what comes after—setting the rows with a tiller—often isn't. Daddy and my brothers were good with a tiller, but I never

Farming was a real challenge in Jackson County, as there just isn't a lot of level land. On the upside, there were places where you could dig potatoes and just let them roll downhill. *Hunter Library, Western Carolina University.*

got the hang of it. When I was five years old, I still believed you could dig to China if you really put your mind to it. I no longer believed that when I was fifteen but almost pulled it off with the family tiller.

Tillers seem to want to do one of four things: not start, not stop, burrow like a groundhog or take off like a startled horse. I've seen more than one person laid out behind one, being dragged along before it dawned on them that they were hanging on by the throttle and should probably just let go. Although with our property, it wasn't certain you'd ever see the tiller again if you left it to its own devices.

In pre-tiller days, the garden rows were laid out by mule. Our neighbor Early Deitz used a mule every spring up into his nineties. The trick to getting a straight row, I've been told, was to pick out a target between the mule's ears and fix on it, sort of keeping it lined up like a gunsight and following to the end of the row. Of course, after getting the first row or two straight, there was no longer a need for that, as you simply followed the plowed paths.

But a lot of people kept sighting between the mule's ears anyway, the consensus being that if you simply looked ahead at eye level, you'd be staring at the less-flattering end of the mule, a view that got old pretty fast.

THE LITTLE EGG THAT COULD...LEAD TO A CAR CRASH

I guess the worst Easter egg hunt I experienced was the one where I wrecked the car.

We had a '55 Chevy that my siblings dubbed the Flinstonemobile. Like most American cars of the era, it was a huge hunk of metal with a huge engine and had enough giddyup to climb a telephone pole. Parts of the Chevy, however, were not made of metal, and those parts evidently were made of particle board. You could see the road zipping by through holes in the floorboard, thus the *Flintstones* reference. It was reasoned that if the car ran out of gas, you could jam your feet through the floor and start running the Chevy to the next gas station. It didn't have many of the safety or anti-theft devices we're accustomed to these days. For example, you could crank it with a nickel.

The car came into play when one Easter rolled around and we were hiding eggs. I discovered that the diameter of this particular batch of Easter eggs matched the diameter of the tailpipe of the Chevy. Not wanting to make the hunt too easy, I went ahead and gave the egg a shove to better hide it in the exhaust system.

When we rounded up the eggs, there it stayed. All attempts to dislodge it just pushed it farther up the tailpipe, where it glowered back at me with an expression that said, "You may well die this very day." Messing with the car was as of big a no-no as there was—capital offense, verboten, bad, bad idea. I had no idea what jamming the exhaust system would do to the car, but I knew it couldn't be good.

With the clock ticking and Mother and Daddy bound to show up at any moment, I did the only thing I could think of: start looking for a nickel.

My recollection of events afterward is very fuzzy. The nickel was obtained and the car cranked. The egg shot out like it had been fired from a bazooka. Now out of gear, the car began lazily rolling backward. Fortunately, one of the metal parts was what made contact after it gained momentum and wheeled into a soft dirt bank.

That I remember. What I can't remember is why I'm still alive. I don't recall if one of my siblings moved the car back into its parking spot or what happened, but somehow, major consequences were avoided.

Now, whuppins were quite common in those days, but while Daddy went for his belt once or twice, he never actually whipped me. That's probably because once he made that motion, I'd be deep in the woods trying to figure out in which direction the Canadian border lay. No, it was Mother, as in the case of many mountain households, who dispatched the discipline.

We had a county fair prize–winning-caliber yellow bell bush out beyond the kitchen door, and one would have to march to it, select a switch and return with it for punishment. Mother was an extraordinarily kind and caring woman and a small person, so she never lashed anyone in a manner that left an impact, but, oh, man did it sting. She'd grab me by one arm, aim for the calves with the other and, as a duo, we'd do a little jig in a circle, with me yelling my head off. From a distance, it probably would have looked like I was in training for *Riverdance*.

But that didn't happen in the Easter caper. I remember getting off clean and only revealing the tale to Mother and Daddy years later. Whatever the case, thanks to whichever sibling bailed me out. You can keep the nickel.

Ramping Up for Easter: Ham and a Mountain Necessity

As the extended Buchanan clan began its preparations for the Easter gathering of 2018, we knew that while the patriarch and matriarch, Mother and Daddy, wouldn't be around, it would still be a sizeable gathering, and lists of who was bringing what were flying around on social media. For Christmas and Easter, I usually provide ham. It's a long-standing tradition that was started in part by my late father-in-law, who'd send my family a Christmas ham, and in part by an old editor friend of mine.

This fellow had a family that would be a bit contentious when it came to arguing over politics and whatnot, but he discovered that hard feelings wouldn't last long if he brought a ham to the proceedings. He called it the "Ham of Atonement."

Ham at Easter is a pretty big tradition in these parts, thanks to the venerable country ham. Growing up, pretty much every farm home had a smokehouse attached or standing free nearby. Although Daddy's smokehouse never saw smoke by the time I came along, it was still used for storage. Smoke went out of style when salt became cheap around the late 1800s, and salt went out of style when freezers became affordable. Still, a few people held on to the smoking art, and a smoked ham was a prized commodity. It could get a family through a winter and would serve as a prized gift for someone atop the giver's list.

There weren't many stories I heard about the smoking process, but it seems everyone had a story about sending a country ham to a greenhorn in the city, only to hear it had been destroyed. See, a well-aged ham will have white flecks in it formed by the aging process, but someone unfamiliar with country ham will mistake that for spoilage. In the garbage it goes.

Similarly, I gather that you must soak a country ham, or you might as well try eating a salt lick. Again, instructions to do so rarely went with a ham delivery. I don't know what the batting average was for a country ham delivery to a person in the big city regarding successful enjoyment, but it's probably around that of a utility infielder for the Atlanta Braves. In other words, not all that impressive. At any rate, "store" hams have largely replaced country hams. They're different, but fine in their own regard.

While ham is dandy, what spring means to mountain folk is a whole different victual: ramps. Ramps have been described as a sort of onion, sort of leek, sort of garlic, but they stand apart from all of those. They're stinky, life-reviving bulbs that grow wild in local coves and hollows, and it just isn't spring without them. I guess they have an affinity for Easter in that their chemical compound is said to help restore the body after a winter without greens.

On the death side of the resurrection equation, they kind of smell like sulfur, so strongly, in fact, that there's still a law on the books in West Virginia that children can't attend school after having eaten ramps. I've heard that a lot of kids took advantage of that in local schools back in the day. Kids know the score.

As with so many other foodstuffs, Mother could cook some ramps 'n taters, and I still miss her fussing over the cast-iron skillet every spring. Still, my sisters picked up her skills well and can turn out a mess of ramps. However, perusing the lists of who's bringing what on text messages, I didn't see that anyone was bringing them to family Easter feed that year.

I thought about issuing a threat: ramps 'n taters or the ham gets it. Atonement comes with a price, you know.

Puttin' Up Time Comes Again to the Mountains

It was almost as if a signal had been sent up. I was on my way to Cherokee as May rolled into June on a hot, dry but somehow steamy day when folks were taking to the waters of the Tuck or Oconaluftee looking for some relief. But not everyone was heading that way. As people streamed to cool mountain waters, farmers were streaming into the fields to make the first cutting of hay.

One of the many things that sets these mountains apart is that unlike the big industrial farming operations across areas of the country where the land is flat, you don't see large tractors with enclosed, air-conditioned cabs. These guys were out there in the elements, perched atop steel pan seats with no relief from the sun but a hat. Technology has changed a lot, but gravity and terrain still hold the trump cards in many mountain fields.

Still, puttin' up hay has changed a lot in my lifetime. What I consider my first real job took place when I was ten or so, chucking loose hay with a pitchfork into the back of Bill Buchanan's pickup truck. I got paid nine dollars and felt richer than any Texas oilman.

Over the years, I've grown nostalgic about putting up hay and all the terminology involved in the practice. You don't store hay, you put it up. And puttin' it up meant using a pitchfork to pitch it into whatever means you had to transport it, and then into a barn loft.

It was quite a trick with loose hay, and pitchforks were specialized. Pitchforks with two tines—the pointy business end—were used to spear hay or any other material that had been gathered up enough to hold together. Three-tine pitchforks, the type you see in the painting *American Gothic*, were for loose hay.

Sometimes the hay was put up by stacking it in the fields, something I haven't seen for many years, which is a shame. Haystacks were awesome playgrounds for kids playing king of the hill or hide and seek. And they were a good place to take a nap. Any kid who's ever enjoyed jumping on a bed would've liked the soft give of a haystack, which offered little danger other than the remote possibility that you might jump on a snake—or back in the Depression era, a hobo.

I think the hay bale probably killed off the haystack and made the pitchfork a curio at antique shops. You still put the hay up but now by slinging it onto a truck and then into the barn. The aforementioned Bill had a love of geometry and could get, if I recall, forty-eight bales onto his truck if arranged just right. At the time, a judge would've had to sentence me to geometry, but Bill showed me all the tricks, and it worked every time.

You still see hay bales in the mountains in some fields, but like the bale replaced loose hay, the small bale has been replaced by those enormous round bales that resemble shredded wheat, only with about a thousand servings per biscuit. Another important difference is that I don't ever recall

Apples laid out to dry for the winter ahead. A lot of folks on East Fork would also string beans—leather britches—to dry in order to have something in the pot come February. A curiosity in mountain language is that you didn't store or save apples, beans or hay. You put it up. *Hunter Library, Western Carolina University.*

thinking a regular hay bale could kill me, but those big boys can weigh half a ton or more and, being round, can roll. Potentially a bad combination right there.

Hay was a lot of hard work, but I do get nostalgic thinking about old-timers in the field talking about whether to winnow or let it lay, various curing tricks and how wet bales could combust and start a fire in the barn.

Still, it's fun to watch the tractors roll and to reminisce, especially when it's somebody else doing the puttin' up.

SOME FUNDAMENTAL SHIFTS IN THE CULTURE

Who Knew Lightnin' Bugs Would Become an Economic Driver?

Some of our interactions with wildlife have definitely taken on a Disney quality. Take, for example, Cataloochee over in the Great Smoky Mountains National Park. I still like going there, but it's changed since the reintroduction of elk to the park. I'll admit they're impressive beasts. Still, I didn't realize they'd be such a game-changer. What was once a rather obscure location is now overrun by throngs of people wanting to see an elk, to the point that it's so crowded you want to go to Walmart afterward to get away from it all and unwind.

We're seeing sort of the same thing with lightnin' bugs (fireflies, if you must). People have begun turning out by the hundreds to see rare sights such as synchronized displays in the Smokies. Lightnin' bugs were made to be caught and put in Mason jars with holes poked in the lid and a little grass scattered in the bottom to light up a dark bedroom. Little did I realize they'd one day be an engine of commerce.

I guess a drawback of growing up here was growing up with the assumption that mountain culture was like culture everywhere else. That this wasn't the case began dawning on me at a young age while watching tourists interacting with the Cherokee. There were several places in Cherokee where you could have your picture taken with Cherokee, who tended to be dressed as Plains Indians from the latest John Wayne film. Some people made a pretty good living at it, and this was at a time when making a living in Cherokee wasn't easy.

Still, it puzzled me to no end, as the practice struck me as akin to someone wanting to have a picture taken with, say, one of my aunts dressed up as a

Hessian. I mean, one of the first things anyone would tell you about the Cherokee, including my Cherokee friends, is that they didn't wear war bonnets and they lived in houses, not tepees.

It was very frustrating, both on an ethical level of seeing bad history disseminated and on the more practical level of not having a piece of the action. A friend and I discussed throwing on overalls and putting up a sign saying, "Have Your Picture Taken with a Genuine Hillbilly!" The idea never gained traction, as it wasn't a very good one.

At any rate, thinking about cultural shifts and reading about the lightning bug hootenannies that are popular now got me to thinking about another summer insect favorite: the June bug. June bugs (actually beetles) pop out around, well, usually July, truth be told. Farmers and gardeners hate them, but kids used to love them.

June bugs are active fliers but not particularly accurate ones. You can hear them banging off the sides of houses, screens or almost any stationary object once they become active. Their navigational skills are pretty much on a par with Otis Campbell driving home after a bender. Still, they're fairly easy to catch, and once you caught one, you could tie a string to one of its legs.

It was educational as all get-out. You learned about what types of string were best suited to June bug roping. Too heavy and the bugs couldn't fly well; too flimsy and they might slip out of the noose. If an electric fence or powerline was nearby, you might pick up a handy lesson on the conductive properties of certain makes of string.

Several of us would get together and capture a number of June bugs with the goal of having dogfights. The visions of exciting aerial combat always ended with a mere tangled ball of string attached to a mass of June bugs feigning death, having figured out that if they quit flying around entertaining us, we'd lose interest. And we did. Because by that time of the day, the lightnin' bugs were coming out.

There's Something in the Air, so Beware

Once the heat of late spring and early summer sets in, one better plan for pop-up thunderstorms in these mountains. Oh, the official forecast may be for "a possibility of scattered thunderstorms" or "30 percent chance of precipitation," but when they deliver, there's nothing scattered or 30 percent about them.

One of my very early memories involved being terrified by a relentless wave of bone-rattling thunder. Looking to reassure me, Mother said something to the effect that the noise was just the sound of dwarves up at the head of the creek bowling. I'll admit, the tale, which probably originated many decades earlier in "Rip Van Winkle," did calm me down. Only years later would I need to seek therapy for my deeply held belief that the woods were filled with bowling ball–wielding dwarfs.

Not really, but the incident with the thunder probably did kick off my lifelong series of misadventures with lightning and, more broadly, electricity.

Electrification was late to isolated pockets of these mountains. I remember Daddy gently prodding an old mountaineer up the creek, telling him to look into getting his house wired and holding forth on the various benefits, such as lighting and cooking without worrying too much about burning the house down. He didn't make the sale. The gent had never had it and figured he didn't need it, and I guess he had a point.

We were warned about the dangers of electricity. I was pointedly told not to stick a bobby pin in an electrical outlet, and I never did, at least after that first try. Our neighbor Bill Buchanan had barely thrown the switch to his new electric fence when I marched down and grabbed it with both hands and had to be yanked off. That was about the point that I quit seeking out electricity. But the thing about electricity here in the hills is that sometimes it decides to seek you out.

The family was on an outing down to a remote stretch of river in the southern part of the county one summer day when a storm blew up out of nowhere. Climbing the hill back to the truck, it took a good number of us out when a bolt of lightning hit the mountainside and spread out, hitting, at the very least, my two brothers, my brother-in-law Mike and me. It rendered Mike numb. Howard and Gary had Prince Albert tins with worms in their back pockets, and the reaction of the tin killed them (the worms). All in all, the experience was akin to how it feels when you hit your thumb with a hammer—only it applies to your whole body.

I had a similar experience years later, involving pushing a metal drill in a metal box under a barbed-wire fence when a bolt hit just about on top of me. It ran down the fence quicker than my mind could react to the fact that I was pushing a metal box with one hand and holding a conductive strand of wire with the other. My brain started out with "LET G—," and the next thing I knew, I was other side of the fence, dazed but not much worse for wear.

My hair was naturally (unnaturally?) curly for a decade or so after that one.

One type of lightning I haven't seen here is ball lightning, but there's a family tale about it. One summer day, the story goes, this ball of plasma just sort of materialized in the living room. It wobbled drunkenly, bobbing around, and eventually veered up the chimney. It floated out of the house and settled a few feet above the well housing out back from the kitchen steps. It hung in the air and exploded with a monstrous thunderclap.

I don't know what set it off. Maybe somebody stuck a bobby pin in it.

I Couldn't Stand the Heat, so I Did in Fact Get out of the Kitchen

Back in the 1970s, winters were colder in the mountains. There were also years when the calendar said summer had just started, but it felt like it was dragging into its seventeenth month. Those summers, things got hot at the Buchanan home on East Fork. Nature and tradition merged in a cruel manner. Beans and whatnot started to hit in the garden, and that meant it was time to start putting away some of the goodies for the hard winter months.

To accomplish the feat, the stove in the cramped kitchen was four-burner blazing most the day. In that kitchen, Mother would turn blackberries into jelly and tomatoes into soup to be consumed next February, and the process of canning enough green beans to feed an army would commence. Given that it was generally hovering around ninety degrees outside, this put the temperature in the kitchen equivalent to the surface of Mercury.

Over the years, I've observed that human beings have a distinct tendency toward turning, shall we say politely, oval in body appearance as they advance in years. I also observed that this didn't happen to a lot of mountain people. In the case of a lot of the men, well, they ate like farmers but they worked like farmers, so it evened out.

Mother remained a small woman all her life. I'm sure a lot of that was virtue—she was never a heavy eater and was a complete stranger to vices—even the fun ones.

But I'm sure the kitchen had a lot to do with keeping her petite. It was like a sweat lodge. One could start having visions of long-departed relatives just by walking through it on the way to the back door. Mother, she stayed in there for hours at a time for weeks on end. It's no wonder the poor woman never had a chance to get heavy. It is a wonder that she didn't simply evaporate at some point.

The canhouse was a mainstay for mountain families and was filled with tomatoes, beans and jellies put up as a food bank against the coming frosts. The act of canning took place in the heat of summer. During that chore, a typical mountain kitchen was as hot as the surface of Mercury. *Hunter Library, Western Carolina University.*

The whole enterprise had a lot to do with a sort of fondness I developed for stringing green beans. I never developed a fondness for eating them, but I found the string and snap work kind of contemplative. Mainly, that contemplation involved whether human combustion was an actual thing or not, and it struck me that maybe such a thing could happen in the canning kitchen. Beans were strung outside on the porch, well away from the kitchen.

Ah, but what transpired in that kitchen was sheer wizardry. The most inexpensive of ingredients turned into items to fill the larder and incredible cakes with the added bonus of bowls to be licked.

Mother sometimes used written recipes but seemed to make up a fair amount of her cooking on the fly. I kind of picked that up from her when it comes to reading directions. As the saying goes, I couldn't pour water out of a boot if the directions were on the heel.

At any rate, it was fascinating to watch the cycle of planting to harvesting to canning. It was a way of life not very long ago because people had to depend on themselves instead of a big box store. Nature is amazing. Plant some beans or corn, and you have not only food but also seed to plant more beans and corn the next year. I stumbled over a Robert Heinlein quote the other day that made me realize the same equation is probably why so many mountain folks stuck by their milk and beef cattle and plow mules and horses long after they could've ditched them for the convenience of the supermarket: "Horses can manufacture more horses and that is one trick that tractors have never learned."

The Garden Ends, Mayhem Begins

One of the sights I enjoyed most in my youth was the browning of the cornstalks in the garden. It was a sign that harvest was winding down, which meant Mother wouldn't be turning the kitchen into a blast furnace much longer.

Mother and Daddy always tried to coax the very last tomatoes of the season off the vines and were a bit sad when only dried stalks of plants remained. On the flip side, after putting up scores of jars of green beans, the general mood toward that part of the garden was "just quit already."

Those dried stalks thrilled me. They meant garden work would soon be over, except for digging up the potatoes in a few weeks. And after that, it would be time to burn the sucker down. We usually burned off the garden in spring, but I vaguely recall doing it in fall at least once. One time we burned at night, which I'm not sure is legal anymore; it might not have been legal then, come to think of it. It made sense to me, as you could easily see what was still flaming and stomp it out. I would run up to the blaze in the crisp night air to warm up, and then dash away.

One time I had a big sheet of asbestos Daddy had brought from a worksite, and I used it like some superhero's shield to keep the dancing flames at bay. I thought it was cool as all get out. I'm really sure that's not legal anymore.

I recently sort of pieced together why the habit of fall burning might have persisted in some sections of the mountains. A lot of it, surprisingly, had to do with worms. I had no idea night crawlers and red worms weren't native until I read Jared Diamond's bestseller *Guns, Germs and Steel: The Fates of Human Societies*. It turns out that they probably showed up when trading ships came to load up on tobacco. The traders would dump ballast in order to take on the load, and that ballast—dirt and rocks—was likely oozing with worms.

Worms eat leaf litter, but as they weren't around to do so in America for millennia, a common practice among Native Americans was to burn the litter off every autumn. I imagine that habit, like so many others, got handed off from the Cherokee to the mountaineers, and we may have been unwittingly replicating it on East Fork for a fall or two. But it was usually a spring fling.

Fire was used to clear land as well, but some land can be stubborn, as was the case with one of my neighbors, who had a tangled mess of vine that seem impervious to scythe and axe. His solution reminds me how times have changed. He turned me loose with a pressure sprayer full of kerosene, lit a small fire in the patch and told me to go at it. I'll admit I had a blast—figuratively, not literally. But looking back, it was pretty irresponsible on the part of my neighbor. He didn't even give me a sheet of asbestos.

THE SEASON OF OMENS AND PORTENTS

It's a curious world and seems to be more curious still when we settle into October, the month of haints, omens and portents here in the mountains. Since I came of age as a lot of traditions in these hills were dying out but weren't altogether gone, I still have memories of people dabbling in somewhat spooky arts.

Water witching, for example. Also known as dousing or divining, a water witch would use a couple of L-shaped branches or rods to locate a good site for a well. In other parts of the country, people might witch for gemstones or try to locate oil or perhaps a relative's abandoned gravesite.

Some people put a lot of stock in dousing. Others, such as one old-timer who was around while a couple of amateur dousers wandered around trying to find a spring in an abandoned field, didn't. This particular graybeard observed that we live in an area that's so lush it would be more impressive to not strike water, and I suppose he had a point there.

Another witching tradition handed down was the practice of tying a pencil on a string and holding it over the outstretched palm of a youngster; the revolutions of the pencil would foretell how many children you'd have, with the direction of the revolution determining how many boys or girls you could look forward to. As it wasn't uncommon in those days for couples to have ten or twelve kids, the prediction would usually be something like four boys and three girls. But at about the same era as the pencil, witching people

Dowsing to find water or a long-lost grave was a common practice in the mountains, along with an entire host of other mystical dabblings. *Hunter Library, Western Carolina University.*

quit having large families, meaning the predictions were generally off by an order of magnitude.

I'm not sure if people were more superstitious back then. It occurs to me that we're still superstitious as all get-out. I'll veer away from a black cat in my path and toss salt over my shoulder if a shaker is knocked over. I won't open an umbrella indoors, and I'll never, ever walk under a ladder.

At least in the old days, superstitions were, for lack of better terms, more charming, or carried more portent. The charming superstitions were four-leaf clovers and rabbit's feet, although it was often pointed out a rabbit's foot couldn't be that lucky, considering what happened to the rabbit.

The omens that carried portent often involved somebody's death. Therein lies a Buchanan family tale. Going back decades, there was a belief that if somebody spotted a white animal—owl, fox, whatever—at dusk, it signaled the oncoming death of a family member. Such a combination of events was documented in the death of an uncle many years back. The tale circulated frequently and was passed down along the generations.

Daddy had been in hospice at the Charles George VA in Asheville for several weeks when he took a sharp turn for the worse, and it became evident that the end was near. Family members took turns sitting with him. I was with him when he peacefully passed. One of my nieces related to me that the night before she'd had a dream where her Maw-Maw came down from the sky riding a snow-white bear to collect Daddy. She loved her man, and he loved bears, so the story was appropriate and fit right in with the family legend.

The thing is, my niece had never heard that particular tale. It's a curious world.

IT SLICES, IT DICES—NO WAIT, IT JUST EMPTIES YOUR BANK ACCOUNT

It's safe to say that a great many Christmas traditions have changed—for example, Christmas lights. I'm not sure it ever took hold here, but the old German tradition saw people putting candles in their trees to imitate stars flickering among the evergreens. Given that fire and tinder-dry trees are natural enemies in the wild, it was a risky proposition. The festivities generally saw the candles lit only briefly as the family sat around with buckets of sand and water.

Electric lights changed that, although in early days, electrical wiring was about as dangerous as an open flame. In addition, the early lights were wildly expensive, running around $12 per string back in 1900, which is around $300 in today's money. Plus, each bulb needed to be wired individually, so the task also involved hiring an electrician. But technology marched on, lights became cheaper, good old American one-upmanship kicked in and, as a result, today many homes can be spotted from orbit.

Another big change is also related to electronics: we now spend inordinate sums of money on technological gifts that go obsolete in about eighteen months. Phones wear out and fall behind, and games wear out and fall behind. The DVD is as dead as the dodo. All of the accessories associated with the upgrades are stored away and turn into archaeological artifacts. What does this cord go to? Dunno, but better not toss it, as it might come in handy someday. Say, to wear as a belt when you're broke from updating your technology.

In doing a little research on Christmas lights, I came across the mother of all technological gifts—one that I'm happy to say nobody in Jackson County purchased. Introducing the Honeywell Kitchen Computer (HKC), also known as the H316 pedestal model. Weighing in at more than one hundred pounds, the HKC was more or less a glorified recipe book. While it came with a few recipes, in theory, you would have to input new recipes yourself. That task required a two-week training course. Afterward, you could spend time playing with toggle switches and a binary-light output—time that probably could have been better spent reading a cookbook or ordering a pizza.

Oh, and the price tag for this wonder of the year 1969? A mere $10,600, or about $71,000 in today's dollars. That sounds steep, but the HKC did come with a built-in chopping board. Like I said, nobody fell for the allure of the HKC here in Jackson County. There's no evidence that anyone on the planet did.

Those boxes of mystery cords we all have in our homes may be an indicator that we've gotten older but not particularly wiser.

Yes, It's Cold, but It Still Beats the Heat

OK, I'll admit it. It's cold. I adhere to a sort of code when it comes to weather: I try my best to not complain about the cold. Before I was born, I apparently took two turns standing in line at the "hot-natured" because

I generally just feel better when the temperatures drop below fifty and keep going.

I save up the complaining about the weather for the heat of summer and, brother, do I ever turn it loose then. That said, I have noticed since I've shot past fifty, the whole "relishing the cold" gift is a bit more challenging. I fear I may not have fully mastered the tactic that my father and forefathers employed when it came to life's little challenges, such as cold weather, unpleasant people and moonshine laws: ignore them.

Mother, on the other hand, didn't care one bit for cold. In her advanced years, she could never keep her feet warm and had a tendency to crank up the thermostat to the point that when you entered the house your glasses would immediately fog up. One Christmas, sister Connie had boiled some potatoes and had dumped the water in the sink by the kitchen door just as brother Howard showed up. I opened the back door to step out and a cloud of steam billowed out the back door. Howard sat there behind the wheel, assuming that cloud was the heat of the house escaping. You could clearly tell he thought pretty hard about just putting the car in reverse and leaving, but he did eventually come in. Connie's potato dish, like everything else cooked by the women of the Buchanan clan, was delicious.

Unlike Mother, I'm always hot, so it's a lot easier to remember the coldest points in my life. On one bear hunt, I didn't bother to take gloves, worked up a sweat climbing a mountain in frigid conditions and found myself with my hands frozen to my rifle. "Now this," I thought to myself, picturing a bear waddling up to me and essentially wearing the equivalent of handcuffs, "would be one stupid way to die."

Another time I had chopped some wood, came in, took a drink of water from the faucet and went back out to collect a load for the stove. It was cold enough that the water in my beard froze, and a chunk of it snapped off. I told everyone I had mange.

The coldest I can recall, though, was in 1985, when I was working in Cashiers. An Alberta Clipper rolled through the area, and I vaguely recall wind chills getting to negative seventy-five degrees. That figure started sounding more and more absurd the older I got, so I looked it up. It was negative thirty-four degrees on Mount Mitchell on January 21, 1985. Grandfather Mountain saw wind chills of negative one hundred. Heck, Cashiers at negative seventy-five was downright balmy compared to that.

So, against this backdrop, a friend of mine in Cullowhee had vacated the clapboard house he was renting to go to the beach (where it was about fifteen degrees), and it was up to me to feed his cats. The place had not even a sheet of paper for insulation, and the power had failed, so naturally everything had frozen. The toilet had shattered. He'd left the faucet dripping, so at least there was water for the cats.

My friend loved his cats, and instead of dry food, he treated them to those big cans of cat food. I opened one, and that goop slid out and landed on the floor with a thump like a frozen Yule log. And like the scene in *A Christmas Story* when the kid takes up the dare to stick his tongue to a telephone pole, I had a cat hanging off each end of the food. I cannot describe the sound.

Luckily, enough water was dribbling from the faucet to remedy the situation. The cats were fine. The toilet was replaced. Life went on. Summer came, and it got hot. I complained about it to anyone who would listen.

Tales of Turkey Terror

If I was asked what I wanted my last meal to be, I'd answer one of the following: Thanksgiving, summer cookout or church homecoming.

Of course, there are other good answers to that question, ranging from Sunday dinner to Homer Simpson's response. He misunderstood the gist of "I would like my last meal to be…" and answered, "Smothered in country gravy."

At any rate, I'd have to come down on the side of Thanksgiving. It's a complex meal, and I was blessed to have a mother and family of wonderful cooks. Thanksgiving would begin around 3:00 a.m. at the house on East Fork. The turkey would be on the counter thawing, and we received no end of lectures regarding how dangerous the thing was. Mountain kids tend to be (a) hungry and (b) grabby, so we were told repeatedly of the exotic fatal diseases one would invite by touching a raw turkey.

I for one treated the thing like a live hand grenade. I wouldn't even look at it sideways. In fact, my first bite of turkey was taken with great trepidation, figuring if it was that deadly, no amount of cooking was going to calm it down. But bite I did. Man, Mother could cook. That first bite began a lifelong love affair.

But turkey's tricky. While I know my way around a grill with ease that is not true when it comes to the bird. I haven't tried turkey very often, but it tends to turn out dry. That's probably a hangover from the salmonella lectures.

I learned most of my cooking skills before I got married, and turkey is not a bachelor dish, mainly because turkey requires patience. I've witnessed and heard of some epic disasters, ranging from giblets being cooked inside the turkey to one instance where one of those pop-up thermometers that shows the turkey was cooked came shooting out and rattled around the inside of the oven like a BB in a soup can. I also heard of one turkey that was engulfed in foam bubbling out of the oven. The instructions to clean the bird were apparently taken literally.

As for the giblets, they tend to be a great surprise package for the uninitiated. Skilled cooks work wondrous stuffing and gravies with them, but for rookies, they're a big slimy bonus gift they had no idea was in the bird. I have no idea what they are, for that matter. It turns out that if they're wrapped in paper, your bird isn't ruined. If they're wrapped in melted plastic, well, you're eating melted plastic. Bon appétit.

Thanks to the talent of Mother and the other cooks gathered for Thanksgiving, we never had a turkey disaster. Well, just one, but it wasn't due to an exploding bird or a giblet misfire. The moment came on this particular holiday when the food was being laid out and tables were groaning with delectable sides. Still more tables were covered with cakes and pies, when a hushed conversation broke out between Mother and a couple of my sisters. Panic was in the air.

See, Thanksgiving meals at the height of the family gatherings were logistical challenges akin to the Normandy invasion. Fifty, sixty, who knows how many people might show up. The groundwork to feed this army began long in advance, with lists of who would bring what and agreement on division of labor.

This year, some of the plans were garbled in translation. So and so was supposed to provide the ham. So and so would bring mashed potatoes, three-bean salad, a pecan pie and a chocolate cake. That year about three different people thought three different others were bringing the turkey. When the reality set in that we were birdless, well, dismay doesn't begin to describe it. It was akin to the "Oh, the humanity" recording from the Hindenburg disaster—a great wailing and gnashing of teeth.

Fortunately, a resourceful sister was able to lay her hands on some precooked turkey, and all went well. It was still a good meal—a really good meal. It was good enough to satisfy most if it had been their last.

Coping (or Not) with the Snows of Old

Snows have become rarer in the mountains in the new millenium, but when they do hit, it affords us a chance to break out winter gear we haven't worn in quite a while and also gives us a moment to reflect on how we dealt with the white stuff in days of old. I can't recall a whole lot of actual winter gear. Sure, most of us had a heavy coat reserved for the colder weather, but as far as items exclusively meant to cope with snow, I don't recall much. There was mink oil for the boots, and, actually, mink oil is about all I can recall. On occasion, someone would remember a tip from a Battle of the Bulge veteran and wrap a newspaper sheet around their torso to retain heat, and on other occasions, a few of us would experiment with wearing plastic bread bags on the inside or outside of our boots.

Aside from that, playing in snow usually meant putting on two pairs of jeans instead of one, a pair of gloves and a toboggan. (The cap, not the sled. That would look stupid. Fashion-wise, it would also clash with the bread bags.)

These plans worked well until contact with actual snow. Paper towels are generally made of paper, but you can buy high-test versions that contain a fabric weave, often made of cotton. Jeans are made of denim. Denim is made of cotton. Ergo, we wore child-size paper towel rolls out there doggedly soaking up snowmelt. As to the bread bags on the feet, there's a reason bread bags are designed to hold bread and not feet. One stick or rock and the bags had the integrity of swiss cheese, although they tended to hold in freezing water remarkably well.

In short order, you'd be packing an extra thirty pounds, muscle responses hindered by the extra weight and the fact that directions from the brain quit reaching the legs because the receptors were frozen over. In our minds, we were frolicking, but I suspect a witness from a nearby ridge might've thought he was witnessing the result of a nerve gas test.

But it didn't matter. There was snow, and snow was glorious. It cushioned your fall, held all sorts of possibilities for recreation and, most importantly, got us out of school. Snow could do no wrong. Early on, Daddy would whip together sleds for us with scrap lumber, but somebody eventually figured out that an inner tube made an ideal sled—faster, bouncier, devoid of fancy extras like steering. We also figured out that if you were to pack down a fresh snowfall as darkness fell, you would awaken to a frozen run capable of accelerating an inner tube like something shot out of a cannon. Therein lies a tale.

I'm going to go short on details in this story for reasons that will become clear. We had established a frozen run on a steep hillside a way from East Fork Creek, and I took it upon myself to give it a test run. After shooting down the run—under a couple of grazing cattle a good thirty yards from the place the run ended, under a fence and into the aforementioned creek—my colleagues began questioning the wisdom of shooting down a luge run with no steering or brakes. A plan was devised: somebody would be stationed at the bottom of the run, braced against the ground and using another inner tube as an improvised brake, sort of like the arresting cable they use on aircraft carriers to keep landing planes from shooting off the deck.

If I recall correctly, I was the somebody who agreed to serve as a makeshift brake. An inner tube shot down the hill, its occupant immediately requesting I stop him via screams of encouragement. I'm proud to say the plan worked brilliantly. When inner tube contacted inner tube, the inbound tube stopped immediately. Physics being what it is, its occupant did not. I'm pretty sure he actually increased speed.

He had come down face-first, and I was facing uphill bracing the tube, and I'm told the ensuing collision rang through the valley. "It was just like them bighorn sheep butting heads," one witness said, adding that bighorn do not in fact "drop like a sack of doorknobs" as a result of the exercise.

I cleared my head and, having witnessed the danger of the sled route, we all went right back to tubing, opting to roll off the tubes to grab the barbed wire fence before we shot into the creek. Safety first.

ORANGE MEMORIES WITH A SIDE OF RICE

Even though they're available year-round, the smell of an orange always reminds me of the holiday season. My first encounter with an actual orange came when I was six or so at a Deitz Memorial Baptist Church Christmas Eve service. Sitting in a pew in the flicker of candlelight in the darkened church, I, along with the other children, was handed a gift bag.

Some years there would be a toy in the gift bag. I recall one year I was given a tractor. This was back in the time when toys weren't made of plastic that would fall apart if you looked at it funny. In this case, the tractor was made of cast iron.

As I'd had a lot of plastic toys, and they generally broke within a week or so, the durability of that tractor fascinated me. You could roll it down a hill or off a cliff, and you could fold, spindle and mutilate it to your heart's

Deitz Memorial Church, the scene of the most memorable Christmases for generations of kids from the lower half of East Fork. *Courtesy Dave Russell.*

desire. It suffered nary a ding. I'm not sure what became of it; I imagine it's buried in the dirt somewhere on East Fork, waiting to be uncovered by a bulldozer clearing a house site. I imagine the bulldozer will have a flat.

Anyway, that year I dug through the bag past the sugar sticks, candy canes and plastic-wrapped peppermints. Well, what have we here? A real orange.

I'd had orange juice, but it was the frozen stuff plopped out of a tube and mixed with water. This thing was different. I puzzled over it a bit. It looked like it came from a tree. For a minute, I thought it might be one of those things you shoot from a tree, like mistletoe or a possum, but then I figured it was picked, like an apple. It was a new experience.

Those were days when commerce hadn't quite gotten the toehold it has on us now, so encounters with new foods happened quite a bit in my youth. I'd heard Mother say she didn't care much for rice, and since she was the cook, we never saw it on the table. My first experience with rice came around the same time as my first experience with an orange. I was handed a bag at a wedding. Not knowing I was supposed to throw it at the newly married couple, I was like, "Hey, rice. Heard of this. Think I'll give it a try."

It was awfully hard and chalky and crunchy and seemed like a lot of work. I didn't see how a man could ever fill up on the stuff without losing a set of teeth. I could see why Mother didn't like it. There was also some bird seed mixed in with the rice. It wasn't bad.

Oranges were different. I liked the frozen stuff from the tube, but the fresh item was different. It was fun to separate in wedges to eat, and the juice from it just tasted better. That juice was obtained from a device called an orange reamer, a contraption consisting of a shallow glass reservoir with a raised glass nub in the middle. Mother was quite good at using one; whenever I tried, all I got was juice on my hands, arms and across the kitchen counter in general, with only about a teaspoon where it was supposed to be.

Years later, I came to realize that the orange in the gift bag was part of a tradition both old and new. The original orange story involved the original St. Nicholas back in fourth-century Turkey. He heard the tale of a poor shopkeeper who couldn't afford dowries for his three daughters. St. Nick chucked three gold balls down the fellow's chimney, where they landed in the girl's stockings hanging by the fire to dry.

Oranges, which are a lot cheaper than balls of gold, took the symbolic place in the tale. Here in the United States, an orange in the stocking might be the only gift for a kid during the Depression, and they were certainly a welcome exotic rarity for kids like me in later years.

The enjoyment of orange juice is directly correlated to its freshness. The frozen stuff is fine, although you'll occasionally come across a batch that sits on your stomach like battery acid. Years back, after spending forty or so straight years in these mountains for Christmas, I wound up in southern Florida for Christmas with the in-laws. My father-in-law procured a couple of gallons of juice from a farmer he knew, and it was a revelation. Smooth, sweet, zero acidity, it made me think maybe spending Christmas in Florida could be a thing for me.

Later that day, when we killed two water moccasins on the same green while golfing, I changed that assessment to "reckon not."

CLOAK AND DAGGER TIME ARRIVED WITH CHRISTMAS

Mother had a sneaky streak. Mind you, as with all her powers, it was only used for good. We'd usually get in the range of three to five presents for Christmas. I knew some families that would have dozens of presents under the tree, but I also knew some families that would wrap a pack of gum just to call it a present and add to the count.

Ours were usually substantial presents—Lincoln Logs or a train with circular track or later on perhaps an electric racetrack.

Speaking of those later presents, Santa had a weird sense of humor back in the late 1960s and early 1970s. I vividly remember the year I got that train, because of Daddy's weird sense of humor, he'd packed my train in a plain box and packed my pair of Christmas pajamas in the train box, and made sure I opened that one first. The depths of my disappointment from opening the pajamas was exceeded by the heights of joy when I found a train in a nondescript box.

The train was a wind-up version, so wound up it was. The train went around the track and around and around. It was like NASCAR without the pit stops or wrecks. Naturally, I soon discovered the train would go just fine when not on the tracks, so it soon had all sorts of adventures running around the house, under beds, off the roof.

Conversely, the electric cars of the era needed to stay on the tracks but refused to do so. It was a minor miracle to see one haltingly stop and go an entire lap around the tracks. More often they'd go careening off, and you'd have to work to get them back in the electric slot. After a bit, the contacts between race car and electric rail would wear off, and we'd nip off a piece of a Brillo pad, glue or tape it on and put it on the track. It was a great way to learn about electricity, as about half the time, the Brillo would vaporize in a puff of smoke, the lights would flicker and the "I didn't do it" would begin in earnest.

We'd be pretty careful about the Christmas presents we asked for. Phase one would be the Sears & Roebuck catalogue, although I don't remember Mother ever ordering toys from it. Phase two would be trips to Sylva to the

Downtown Sylva circa 1920. As East Fork was five miles from Sylva, we usually only went there on an occasional Saturday to shop in Jackson County's commercial hub. An exception was Christmas, when Daddy would sneak Mother into town to buy toys, which she carefully wrapped and hid. Finding them prior to December 25 became a bit of an obsession. *Courtesy* Sylva Herald.

five & dime and the drugstores, which were well stocked with toys and pretty much everything else back in those days.

Somehow Mother, who didn't drive, would manage to make it out and back with a haul of toys and other presents without being caught red-handed. And that's where the sneaky part came in—strictly out of necessity. The toys had to go somewhere before being placed under the tree on Christmas morning, and I had one sibling with the search abilities of a bloodhound and the tenacity of a bulldog. Those presents would be found. Some years they weren't; some years they were. If they were, the tape might be picked at for a glimpse. Mother was a good taper, though.

The scene often involved careful handling of the gift, checking it for heft versus volume. It was sort of like that scene in *Raiders of the Lost Ark* where Indiana Jones sits there rubbing his chin, trying to deduce how much sand to put in the bag before switching it with the golden idol on the booby-trapped stand.

I'm not sure we achieved much success in determining who was getting what for Christmas. Mother didn't put name tags on gifts until Christmas morning, as she memorized whose was whose by style of wrapping paper alone. The whole thing was an inexact science. After all, history had already shown there might not be a train in that train box.

THE POWERFUL PULL OF MOUNTAIN HOME

The holiday season is a time when thoughts turn toward home. In these mountains, *home* is a powerful, powerful word. It often means roots that run so deep that they become lost in the soils of time. As such, the home of these mountains has a powerful pull—one that continues to issue a tug, even to families who moved long ago.

As far as I can tell, aside from the upheaval of World War II, the most significant migrations from this area occurred when logging jobs ran dry here and when Detroit ran hot in the postwar era. Droves of mountain folk headed out to where the big timber still stood—the forests of Oregon and Washington—and many are still there.

One of my closest friends from college, a Vietnam-era, two-tour marine sniper, who was taking advantage of the G.I. Bill, lives in Sedro-Woolley, Washington. He observes that the area resembles these mountains and that it's covered with Jackson County names. As I recall, he counted at least three

Buchanan Road/Lane/whatever locations within a few miles of where he lives. I still have cousins out there, and they still remember home.

Detroit's a different story. After his stint in the U.S. Navy during World War II at a flight training base in Florida, Daddy came home and married Mother, Brittie Mae Deitz, and moved around a bit. He did work at the naval base at Norfolk, Virginia, and on projects around Washington, D.C. At one point, he took a job in Detroit, lured, as many here were, by the jobs offered by American manufacturing at its apex. The city of that era was filled with people seeking jobs, to the point that there were nooks and crannies of communities filled with folks from small towns like Sylva, North Carolina.

Daddy didn't care much for Detroit and didn't have a lot of stories about his time there. I do recall two, though. Daddy was a bit rough around the edges, as was common with mountain folk of the day, and on occasion would drop by a Detroit saloon that catered to such men. One night a fight broke out, and an acquaintance of Daddy's, who shall remain nameless, got into a mix with another gentleman.

The two did not exchange words. I'm not sure they even exchanged punches. This particular product of Jackson County decided to dispense with showy moves and got straight to the point, chucking his opponent through the establishment's plate-glass window in a scene that would have been at home in a 1950s Western. Daddy was mixed up in this event in some form or fashion and was a bit concerned there might be consequences, but he got tied up in the pressing business at hand (i.e. making sure there wasn't another combatant, given that plate-glass windows were all over the place in Detroit in those days).

Before the brawlers were able to clear out, a couple of constables did show up. The patron of the establishment pointed out Daddy and his friend and proceeded to give a rousing observation of the relative worth of southern mountain hillbillies versus the rest of humanity. It turns out he came down on the rest of humanity's side. Also turns out that the two cops were from a little village called Sylva, North Carolina. As a result, two other people from Sylva walked away that night without so much as a fine or even a firm "please do not throw customers through windows" talking-to.

The other story is quite brief. Daddy had a sixteen-gauge shotgun he used literally all the way up to his death, a single-shot beast with a kick and a report that would bruise and deafen a person. He found it in a garbage dump outside Detroit. He figured it was probably a murder weapon, but hey, it worked. Over the years, it sent quite a few squirrels to the squirrel maker in the sky.

It's still in the family. Here at home.

About the Author

Jim Buchanan is a Jackson County native and graduate of Sylva-Webster High School and Western Carolina University. He is a longtime mountain newspaperman. He served as editor of the *Cashiers Crossroads Chronicle* before a thirty-year stint with the *Asheville Citizen-Times*, where he last served as editorial page editor. Winner of numerous North Carolina Press Association awards for editorial and column writing, he currently serves as special projects editor for the *Sylva Herald*, where he writes the weekly history page. He serves as a board member of the Western North Carolina Historical Association.

Visit us at
www.historypress.com